# Surviving Another Somerset Year

## CHARLES WOOD

HALSGROVE

First published in Great Britain in 2009

Illustrated by the author.

Also by Charles Wood:
*How to Survive in Somerset*
*Charles Wood's Somerset Quiz Book*

British Library Cataloguing-in-Publication Data
A CIP record for this title is available from the British Library

ISBN 978 1 84114 967 7

**HALSGROVE**
Halsgrove House,
Ryelands Industrial Estate,
Bagley Road, Wellington, Somerset TA21 9PZ
Tel: 01823 653777    Fax: 01823 216796
email: sales@halsgrove.com

Part of the Halsgrove group of companies.
Information on all Halsgrove titles is available at: www.halsgrove.com

Printed and bound by Cromwell Press Group, Trowbridge

# Naming of Parts

# ACKNOWLEDGEMENTS

"Writing is like prostitution," wrote Moliere in the seventeenth century. "First you do it for love, and then for a few close friends, and then for money." I've yet to reach stage three.

However, my gratitude goes out in our economically challenging times to Steven Pugsley at Halsgrove for keeping faith in education, knowing there's more to Somerset life than eels, cider, withies, the balderdash of Kings Alfred and Arthur, and rather a large music festival.

Humungus thanks also to Joan and all at Sarno Square in Abergavenny for their unceasing hospitality in giving me space to reflect, to Mark, Michael, Patrick and Phil for their quiet encouragements in unearthing seductive Somerset secrets, and to Ray for allowing me to rod dangle gainfully for hobbit sharks over the side of his wave conquering little boat.

Closer to home I can only give my heartfelt gratitude to Alina for her love and stoic support in my pursuing a pastime of keypad tapping.

And a mention for Bilbo my reliable snuggle-cat for keeping the author's feet warm from winter's chill under-door draughts.

# NEW BEGINNINGS

*"Every new beginning comes from some other beginning's end."*
Seneca (Roman philosopher, mid-1st century AD)

I've had a soft spot for Somerset's border outpost of Churchinford for a few years now. Its 'York Inn' hints at cricket balls squeezing under willow bats on summer evenings. And my local news had lifted the dark mood on the terrace of the Filmmakers Union during a Human Rights conference in Moldova's capital, Chisinau, a city without street lighting. This was the place of Pushkin's romantic satire, sunflowers and wasp-waisted women. My home boasted the drug-addicted fantasies of Coleridge, stitchwort, honey monsters and the Frome zoologist who felt the need to write the 'Teach Yourself Guide to Sex'.

Cultural differences had become clear even before delegates lunched on fatty pork.

The morning had been spent watching the heartrending. One-minute films made by the country's children who'd grown up too quickly. They had voiced common problems like Aids or being home alone coping with their parents' economic migration from this, Europe's poorest country. A synergy of lingering images of discarded dolls and young teenagers cutting the hair of younger siblings as sad music played. Slogans like "Mother why do you send us toys from Italy? We want you," had produced journalistic tears. The one videoed beside a sun-spangled stream, by a one-handed girl wanting to fly away like a bird, did it for me. There had to be an antithesis.

Cue Churchinford farmer Ken Hunt's tractor-roof nesting wrens. The headline in the *County Gazette* had been "Ken's Tractor is a

Hatchback". The aged farmer had no idea he had uninvited guests as he drove hither and thither collecting hay from his fields. He only noticed their presence when a piece of straw hung down from the roof. A closer look revealed three eggs. When the eggs hatched, mum and dad wren flew to-and-fro food foraging, shouting "tit-tit-tit" at one another while their hatchlings enjoyed rides.

"Ah, he must be a rich farmer," asked Dimitru. "Here we only have horses."

"But, at least yours are useful," I said. "Ours just chase rags."

The conference organisers seemed perplexed as the afternoon session began with chuckles.

So for me in the breaths of winter, the sealed polythene bags of pork meat and sausages labelled 'Beech Hayes Farm, Churchinford,' sold at Taunton farmers market had certain kudos. More so, as the meats were being flogged from a trestle-table by farmer Nick Strange. He looked very similar to David Bellamy, the botanist and broadcaster who I thank for getting me off my bum at a tender age and out discovering the countryside.

Nick was maybe younger and slimmer than David, but was still a rosy-cheeked, fuzz-bearded chuckle-bundle. I got out my wallet for the third time that morning. I had regretted my first impulse, the taste of duck bought from the miserable guy with the spit-outable pies, but had quickly recovered my good humour. Inside my 'bag for life' were a couple of jars of chutney made in the garden shed of the nice, pickle-enthusiast lady in a bobble-hat and scarf.

With the House of Commons and Big Ben having recently topped a poll to find the seven wonders of Britain, Nick and I shared some after-sales repartee about the state of our blunders. It became clearly apparent that he sold his meat countywide. "Clevedon Pier," he said. "The Victorian one didn't last, so why rebuild it? Portishead's a pain in the arse. Thousands of homes and only three roads out. Tesco's Nailsea store rhymes with eyesore. And, why so many hills beyond Weston, on the M5? It could have followed the valley which would've been nicer for the grockles who spend their summers there. Oh, and the traffic lights on Taunton's Silk Mills bridge…"

A voice beside me distracted Nick in full flow. "Hi Charles."

It was Jilly, a woman who makes serious connections. She had introduced me to my wife. "Jilly! How are you? You look …bouncy," I blurted, taken aback by meeting someone I knew. And as an after-thought, to explain my presence beside Nick's meats, added, "I'm touting."

"Well. I'm buying. And that's much more important," said Jilly.

"Don't know about that," said Nick, putting my card somewhere safe.

But that had been yesterday.

Overnight my family, I and the cat were forced to adopt a siege mentality. Beyond the blue, warped front door, Wiveliscombe, or Wivey as it's more affectionately known, had become isolated by snow blizzard. A whiteness that settled in a pig's whisper. And up in the hills a single beech, less impressive than most, toppled to sever the town's power supply. Somerset became like the Victorian world of *Lorna Doone's* creator, Richard Dodderidge Blackmore where, "All the birds were in one direction, steadily journeying westward, not with any heat or speed, neither flying far at once. All we had in snowy ditches were hares so tame that we could pat them, their great black eyes seemed to look at any man for mercy and for comfort." The hairs I patted were those of the cat.

My patio olive tree in a half-barrel tub became an arboreal Quasi-modo. With schools closed children lay on their backs making snow angels in the churchyard. And the town's steep streets were, to coin Boris Johnson's phrase from east of Frome, 'grit-snow lasagne'.

From Smoky Bottom to Bell Hill and Wayford Woods to Holnicote, the snows were the worst for thirty years. The doormat, bereft of the daily arrival of bills, was uncluttered save for the odd slush damp leaf. This got me thinking of a notice of true commitment somewhere along New York's 33rd Street on the wall of the US Post Depot: "Neither snow, nor rain, nor heat nor gloom of night stays these couriers from the swift completion of their appointed rounds." On mentioning this to the postman caught frolicking with his dog, I heard that letter sorting in Wivey post office was impossible without light.

Then again, nothing worked. The hardware store opened for emer-gencies, but with candles and primus stoves soon selling out, shut again. The Co-op closed for three days. And with cash machines dead, Mike Thorne the butcher, lucky with a generator, logged purchases in an 'honesty book' for "payment when possible." But he was soon forced into rationing. So, too, the Spar shop, outside which folk queued to be served with milk, bread and eggs over milk crates placed in the doorway. The store itself was as dark as a cave. A stooped, grey-haired chap said it was like the war. I said it was like Moldova. The public-spirited chopped at pavement ice with spades while others like myself jaywalked, passed by ladies on skis.

As Gill next door began removing snow with a gardening rake from the windscreen of her Skoda, and I began with a Le Creuset spatula on a heap of my own, the snow drops began again. At half-past-four the church clock stopped and time became chimeless in a crow-silent world where Felix, my youngest son, built a snow-ram by torchlight, using curly carrots as horns.

He was an inspiration. The best thing for me to do was to duvet snuggle and dream of book tapping, slipping into sleep repeating the monotonous 'hant-tant-tothery', the curious rhyme once used by Somerset shepherds for counting flocks. At least there was sausage and chutney for breakfast.

Hant, tant, tothery ...

Wiveliscombe 2009.

## HANT
# COW NESTS & EXCUSES

*"There is luxury in self reproach. When we blame ourselves, we feel no one else has a right to blame us."*

Oscar Wilde (Irish Poet, Novelist, Dramatist and Critic, 1854-1900)


Evolution has created a dangerous world, a mix of nettles and brambles, adders and wasps, and creatures of pad, hoof and claw 'going' where they please in a world bereft of picnickers. It's been nearly a hundred-and-fifty years since the noted diarist Rafe Leycester scribbled about "rattling sorts of girls, jolly and well developed" eating al fresco in Wivey where he had "a very sumptuous repast with numberless quart cans of cream into which huge spoons were recklessly plunged and then emerged with their rich loads leaving behind them cavernous holes."

These days our pampered youth stays at home. Apparently, curing boredom amid our rustic charm requires self-motivated ingenuity and the ken to consort with plasma orientated gadgetry.

Success has become a virtual aim of many. Call it progress. Indeed, behind an Axminster bedroom door a fifteen-year-old lad recently became the world champion in virtual guitar, on-line. Not able to play a real guitar, he played 'plastic', pressing the right coloured keys at the right time, and had practiced 40 hours a week, getting up at 0200 BST daily to compete in different time zones. His mother told reporters, "He's really good – a grade A student – I have no worries about him at all."

Opinion is subjective, yet indicative of change and it has always been so. Good to remember then that the compulsion to make one's own entertainment has consequences and rash statements are best avoided. Take, for example, the squire trapped in a pub who lost his two tenanted Ilminster farms on a wet-day wager between a couple of flies having a windowpane race. Call him a twit, but the dubious moral of having fun at the expense of others shouldn't be applauded.

Sometimes though, opportunities are just too good to miss.

"Y'ant coom up yur to get to Parlock?" asked the wrinkled woman with some astonishment at the top of Church Steps on Minehead's North Hill. Being reassured that I really knew this to be a very indirect route, she abandoned the sarcasm she was prepared with and was reduced to satirising 'fornas' in general. "Some on 'em doan' niver think of asking the way. They jest goos arn, an' then they goos wrong. I often larfs in me sleeve at 'em, I do." Dear old baggage, I thought, such stuff's being going on for years.

Before rural Somerset got telly and plastic cartons and the mantle of gullibility passed to grockles, few owned-up to teasing the evacuee kids from the London Blitz oblivious to where milk came from. Still in living memory, youth had innocence and local pranksters reduced themselves to laughter stitches. Without hesitation, the unworldly-wise regularly believed that a cluster of milk bottles in the hedgerow was a cow's nest.

Happily, Joan Rolfe, the seventh of thirteen children, still recalls the hedgerow planting.

Her dad was a cowman who, too, witnessed a disturbing change in natural selection. After the war the buzz-word was 'artificial insemination', and the pin-striped fellow from 'The Ministry' turning up with a large syringe at the farm gate was of concern to yokel and bull alike. Several months after 'a visit' Joan's dad came running up the garden path, 'all a-lather'. "Daisy's 'ad twins," he had gasped, "An' their father wore a bowler 'at."

During the 1960s, Courage, by way of brewing rather than fortitude, brought Joan and husband Ron to live in a Scotch Horn Way bungalow facing the grey stone ruins of Nailsea glassworks. They had closed in 1873 – a forty-year story of boom to bust that had seen Nailsea Glass being one of the four largest glassworks in the country to 'zip' as coal supplies dwindled. Flasks and bottles, jugs and mugs, paperweights and twisted canes, rolling pins and pipes, are now prized collectables. Today, only a pair of large ceramic murals by Ned Heywood depicting local glass history on the side of Nailsea's Tesco and the 'Friendship Inn', built specially for the glassworkers almost opposite 'the Royal Oak,' Wurzel Adge Cutler's favourite local, are all that remain of that Somerset Murano.

Grockles seem oblivious that Somerset folk weren't always just yokels in smocks, gob dangling straw.

The council turned the glassworks into a cats' paradise of a park in front of Joan's eyes.

This gave her Siamese tomcats, wise Havoc and young Tuppence, options. Either they could do their thing on newly manicured lawns, or stick to the rough acres of adjacent Brockway Farm from which came distressing night sounds as veal calves were taken away to slaughter. Farmer Brock daren't do it in daylight as the sun would have hurt the calves' eyes. "A tiny bit of consideration at the wrong time of their lives," Joan mused.

Havoc and Tuppence's comings and goings were made possible by Ron's labour of love. Because Joan didn't want cats in her kitchen the Rolfe's was probably the only home in Somerset with a mahogany cat flap and tunnel under the stairs. But only after Ron broke several drill bits, drilling through walls and cavities.

Yet, there was a family sentiment that Ron's design was a mite excessive. A Sunday morning saw Joan discover a ruffled specimen of a fine cock pheasant coming up the stairs. Her shout was met by her son, calling from under the blankets, "Mum, put the gin away and go back to bed."

Despite being a hunt master himself, Havoc was a bad teacher and failed dismally in tutoring Tuppence. Joan had a bin brim full of Tuppence's trophy rubber gloves collected from neighbours' gardens when tools were downed and backs turned for cuppas. It was a habit, or perhaps fetish, Joan first noticed on seeing Tuppence slinking across the park with "something pink" in his mouth. A sense of guilt gave her the ruse to hold a drinks party. The 'glove mysteries' were solved as invited folk deep-rooted to match missing pairs.

For her part, Joan knew that honesty was always the best course. Childhood fibs, although fun, were frowned upon. It was the same elsewhere. The bell inscribed 'From lying lips and slanderous tongue, good Lord deliver us', continually bangs along with the other clamorous bim-boms in Wivey church tower. The church clock, however, recently struck 'Fourteen'. Something worrying had happened. Quiet chunterings that we were beginning to take life too seriously prompted me to rummage in the kitchen cupboard for a pinch of salt and scratch my noggin.

I made a decision. For a couple of hours I left concerns behind me. Heading out from behind my warped blue front door and into my aged car, I was off, waving at Gill, my neighbour, teaching Alexander Technique to Bilbo my adopted street cat before her pottery class. Then down the lane passed the allotments where folk chattered over slug-chewed cabbages before turning left by the school of lost innocence where my children, Lawrence, Maddy, Ez and Felix learned the mantra "Balshy good. Study bad." And away following the road through the woods where dormice dozed, where rooks had been bred for pies and hen pheasants dither with dottiness. I was heading towards the hills topped by Wellington's crumbling bayonet-shaped monument.

My need to apportion blame was nothing new. I had done it before after my Greek born Latin teacher, Mr Athanas, long ago put the words "amor meus Somerset" into my impressionable bonce. Now the world had become an even odder state of affairs. A point made when I bumped into Alan, a young Scot from Troon. He had successfully replied to an ad from 'a Minehead engineering company'. On hearing the pronounced accent, the obvious question posed by Les, the boss of David Naill & Co, was "Do you play the pipes?" Alan took it as the joke he'd heard many times before.

"No."

"Shame, I only ask because we're bagpipe makers. The best."

However, this was a minor detail of outside influence. There was a much bigger one illustrated by John Deere tractors chugging muddy lanes, steered by farm lads sporting baseball caps in harmony with Somerset youth whose iPods play rap. Everywhere CCTV blow secrets, Maccy D cartons catch the wind, and students sip their Starbucks. The meddling that enabled such delights to arrive from America, it's suggested, was local to Yeovil.

A clue to how this influence began can be gained from listening to 'Big 'Ead', a witty ditty written by John Christie and Pete Lawrence, and a Wurzels classic:

"Back in 1497 John Cabot said to his Dad
I think I'll go and discover A'miricle 'cos times is looking bad'.
'Course I'll have to borrow a couple of quid,
Some clothes, and your old top hat
'cos the 'at I got is ten years old
And been sleep in by the cat."

"Okay. And?" you say. Well, things become clearer by adding historical detail. To begin with, the song was about the Bristolian explorer John Cabot going off to discover the familiar. This would not have been possible without an Edwardian butterfly collector and

a chap who had lived in a Camel. Although something of a confused anecdote, many now accept, it was through their efforts that
America got its name. On reflection, it certainly has more of a ring
to it than 'Brendania', after Brendan, the sainted Irish emigrant, who
apparently discovered Yanky-doodledom eight centuries before
Cabot. Timing is everything, and so it proved in Somerset's county
of camels.

For safety reasons, ignore the two statuesque camels beside the M5
at Bridgwater reminding us that more mobile ones had plodded the
Quantocks. Instead, pay attention to one of the two that are places,
the West rather than the Queen. It's West Camel that's known for its
personality. Called Richard Amerike, he was a character able to boast
a notable family tree upon which Queen Elizabeth II, and Diana,
Princess of Wales are out on limbs somewhere.

When Cabot's voyage of discovery to Newfoundland in 1479 was
first proposed, Amerike donated more money than anyone else to
fund the construction of the famous ship, *The Matthew*. As no timber
was readily available nearby, oaks from Amerike's family estate were
cut down and donated. He was also helped to pay John Cabot's
pension.

And the butterfly collector? Well, he was from Bristol and called
Alfred Hudd. It was he who put forward the theory that the word
'America' evolved from Amerike, a plausible suggestion to dispel the
rumour of America being named after a Florentine map-maker.

Nice if the Yanks believed it. Word association isn't rocket science.
And if further proof was needed, Richard Amerike's coat-of-arms
features a stars-and-stripes design.

The lady behind the counter in a bookshop down a Taunton
alleyway said she already knew this interesting stuff, puffing out my
ego flame. Seeing me crestfallen, she was quick to add that many
people probably didn't know. Then again with our Maccy D and
Starbuck culture, their caring about it was a matter of degree. It
wasn't really a hot topic like for instance sheep rustling or a herd of
cows stuck in River Parrett mud having to be pulled out by firemen
aided by 'The Spirit Of Lelaina' and 'The Light Of Elizabeth', a brace
of Somerset hovercraft. Folk liked the weird and wonderful.

After a moment's hesitation, I confided in her a suggestion that I
should write a sequel to the previous book on Somerset that I'd
written.

Despite her knowledge of Amerike, she advised with a winning
smile, "Go for it. We've sold eleven copies of yours in a fortnight, not
bad for a little bookshop."

"You got the rush," I said, keeping to myself a chat with Bob, the County archaeologist, who wears a deerstalker that makes him look like Deputy Dawg. He had warned me that publishers were a bunch of toughies driving hard bargains. Mine could see me coming, a rabbit without a smoot-hole.

"It's bound to be a rubbish contract," I whinged.

"Publishers are like that," she said, still wearing the smile. "They profit from labours of love. And anyway remember *Lorna Doone.*" She had a point. Books have strange fortunes.

The one that put Exmoor on the map had been 'in the bargain bin', deader than a Python parrot, until fate took a hand after R. D. Blackmore's sympathetic publisher, well aware that RDB loved his Lorna, declared, "She shall have another chance. We have lost a lot of money by her; I don't care if we lose some more."

RDB acknowledged his luck in the preface to the twentieth edition, "The dear, dunderheaded add-two-together-and-make-them-five British public came to the wholly erroneous conclusion that 'Lorna Doone' was in some way connected with the marriage of Queen Victoria's fourth daughter the Princess Louise with the Marquess of Lorne; an event which took place in 1871. The times were remarkable for the strong wave of anti-monarchical feeling then rising, in consequence of the recluse life led by the Queen in her widow-hood; and there can be no doubt that 'Lorna Doone' was, in the first instance, purchased so freely because it was suspected of being one of the many scandalous satires then issued in plenty and bought eagerly."

So really one can always have hope for better things. It was the bookshop lady's fault that I was heading for the hills with niggling concerns about poverty outweighed by a zealous love of Somerset. A dangerous cocktail. I knew in my heart-of-hearts not to bite the hand that feeds, nettle soup is so seasonal.

The place I was headed to is still thought of by the odd local or two as 'The Farm'. Indeed, drive between the timber gateposts, and a few stone outbuildings still bless the eye. Not so geese and pigs. There aren't any. Where once hens laid eggs now commerce lays foundations. Bull-bars hereabouts are attached to corporate four-by-fours, and muck gets wiped from the occasional Bentley.

On a concrete-slabbed roadway to sheep, fork-lift trucks joust with articulated lorries, and the likes of me drive very slowly, pallet-splinter watchful. Rumour had it that one young lad handled his fork-lift with the same dexterity he used when out rabbit lamping in his sod-encrusted and battered Fiesta.

After parking in front of a large warehouse built with walls of grey metal I went to a glass paned door with a push button intercom, of the type into which it's fun to shout, "ello!"

Once inside, a suited affable chap shook my hand.

After a discussion whether the office sofas were faux leather or real and the cost implications to authors, the affable chap and I got down to the nitty-gritty. "So, as before I'm to have the book ready while the nasturtiums are still in flower?" I queried.

"Yep. We'll pop you a contract in the post. Standard terms."

I had every hope of surviving another Somerset year. There had been no hint that I couldn't talk about myself just a little bit. If the Latin teacher was not culpable, the bookshop lady certainly was. As I said, I needed to apportion blame as I set off to rediscover puggle-headed bibblers, hobbits and Hairy John, and hopefully many a new acquaintance. Certainly the timing was right. Changes are afoot unseen in Glastonbury's mystical mists.

From upon high church towers the hunky punks are screaming.

Yet, the owls still hoot, dormice snooze, and badgers bulldoze. Spiders remain the webmasters and deer taste yummy. As ever, dumbledores sting, river trout are ticklish, sea fishing is pollocks, and grockles, bless them, are flummoxed.

Through snow siege, by way of primrose and purple heather, to cidrous apple press, local history, like many a burrowing creature, is always there for unearthing, with opportunities arising to put a few things straight, like for instance that Queen Camel.

First though, I had to negotiate the prongs on the forklift driven maniacally by the rabbit lamper, and maybe pop some milk bottles back in the hedge. Rather that, than pick up a plastic guitar or worry on publishers caring about losing money.

## TANT
# HURRYING SLOWLY

*"Rumour is not always wrong."*
Publius Cornelius Tacitus (56 –117, senator and historian of the
Roman Empire)

Rumour had it that the BBC had made an announcement in these hard times. There was a possibility of it sharing news coverage with ITV. Local news had decreasing or little value. True. What benefit can be attached to the story of empty Somerset wallets other than the social? Behind the warped blue front door, although my children seemed suddenly to have grown into adults, the word 'adult' being cautionary, my wallet remains afflicted by a nervous twitch.

Newspapers, cash cows with the news squeezed in, dependent on revenue from houses for sale and let, car sales, and jobs, had seen it fall off a cliff. Yet local news has a place. People like their copy of the *West Somerset Free Press*, the *Burnham & Highbridge Weekly News*, *Bridgwater Mercury*, the *Yeovil Express*, and others of the ilk. The 'take-in-cut-out-and-pass-on' snippet culture is part of Somerset keeping in touch. Issues are important. It's sad that the old-school down-at-heel, chain-smoking, pub-drinking reporters are thinning. Hair implants defy recession for those on the patch.

Advice is to look 'on line' for the news. So, I do. What I see is a drip, drip until the rain stops, then blimey, the pigeons are mating and the line's going boing-de-bounce. Technophobia is an enlightening thing. Loosing community focus must not be blamed on the cider. Folk want to know what's going on in the next street, not ten miles away. That's still foreign news.

And what future is there for Somerset's laptop twiddling youth? For them it's a Facebook world of cyber dudes, to the detriment of local knowledge.

From a farm cottage in the shadow of Dunkery, a few yards beyond the barn where the GPS signal ends abruptly, Mark, my 'on-the-ball' No.1 researcher had sent an email pointing me towards an obscure website where the youth of Somerset had found voice. The words posted were not particularly encouraging:

"Somerset is nearly five minutes wide as the crow flies. Somerset's chief exports include cows, cow produce, agriculture, cow smells and cider. When it rains in Somerset the result is usually blue or green, with some discolouration around the edges of the drops. Although most of the rain goes downwards, a small amount goes by bus."

Although there were elements of wisdom, even one in acne years should surely know that a crow would have to flap faster than a roaring Yeovilton Harrier to cross the county in three hundred seconds. And the bird would miss so much if it did. My youngest son, Felix, eighteen, and still at home with big hair, and snob yob 'Jack Wills' striped shirts had such a loathing of buses that he begged a car able to compete with the website crow, while promising never to use the potential. Not convinced, I paid for something sensible to pootle gently in a world of wonder. A world in which a Dunster beach hut, described by Minehead estate agents as "reminiscent of the post-war holiday years of the 1940s and 1950s," can sell over £70,000. Hell's teeth, back then one could have bought the whole of West Somerset for that amount.

There is a saying in our house: 'Hurry slowly.' I abide by it. Run-along-a-ding-ding is not the Somerset way. It's a waste of time in a county of disunity. We still await an official flag. Councils in Weston and Bath remain bloody-minded and fly their own, both having Avon hangovers. The motto 'Sumorsaete Ealle', meaning 'all the men of Somerset', remains a dream. So, like everyone else, I muddle through.

On wet days an easterly wind drove water between chimney and roof tiles causing the attic squirrel to re-home itself, abandoning the more resilient starlings. The paint on the warped blue front door was peeling. The smooth dip in the doorstep of ancient bricks, eroded by more than a century of footfalls of comings and goings, seemed more pronounced than ever due to the gregarious nature of modern youth. The chill wind blew through the deepening void between door bottom and bricks with the bluster of an unwelcome guest making me whack up the thermostat and feel the pinch.

It's not just me. *The County Gazette* shockingly reported that I was in great company, and suffering from the buzz words 'fuel poverty'. It's epidemic. Sixteen thousand households spread between West Somerset, Taunton, West Somerset and Bridgwater have it, making the area one of the worst affected in the South West. A household gets the tag if it needs to spend over 10 per cent of its income on fuel to maintain a satisfactory heating regime. I dream on, whilst also being told I'm being called 'Fred'; a buzzy acronym meaning, 'Forgotten, Ripped-off, Excluded and Debt-ridden.' A bit harsh, I'd say.

From the street, the combined effect on the eye of blue warped front door and brickwork is aesthetically pleasing, particularly when framed on one side by climbing hydrangea and on the other by rambling rose and intrusive ivy. Readers of *Country Life* call this character. Rustic charm is almost reason enough to curb whinging about bills, almost.

I encountered inner darkness when a little waterfall became a regular rainy weather feature running down the upstairs landing wall, exacerbating the damp rot in the floorboards and making the electrics shocking. At my wife's insistence it was a case of sod the cost. Even if I had to charge Bilbo the cat rent, I decided a watertight roof would be nice. When that was going to be I wasn't quite sure.

An answer-phone message of Somerset burr left me none the wiser. "Hello, Mr Wood. Jerry the Roofer. Just checkin' if it's al'righ' to come out. Oi can't remember if you said you weren't going to be there. If you're not going to be there oi'll try again later, if you're not there, oi'll take it that you're not going to be there and oi won't bovver, an' oi'll try again tomorrow." I decided I would just scratch my head and go with the flow.

To be fair, Jerry turned up with his lad a few days later after Felix had found a 'snow elf' wearing white baseball cap, white trainers and white hoodie, standing in front of him in the Co-op queue, that he labelled with prejudice, "the chaviest chav in the land." Felix was a little taken aback when within an hour, the elf called down to him from the ridge tiles, 'Hi, oi'm yer roofer'. And he and his Dad were golden ones. As autumn closed in, humour behind the warped blue front door became dry, and Felix spoke less judgmentally. "The snow elf wasn't a proper chav, Dad. He drank your Earl Grey tea."

On the occasions Bilbo detached herself from her willow-weaved basket by the radiator. If not encouraging street tickles by looking cute sunning her crotch, she persisted in comforting mourners during final graveside farewells. Such social gatherings occur regularly in the cold weather. So much so that the parish has invested funds in a tough little mechanical digger to assist the stoic mortal ones. I don't mean the moles that seek bijou accommodation in buried craniums, but the former landlord of Wivey's 'White Hart Hotel' and his wife who had wanted a career change. Something down to earth.

When not 'on the lash', Lawrence, my eldest, likes earth, too. Particularly when soil becomes muddy ooze. Taking army leave, he made me a spectator, as he hitched a ride with the scuffle crazy. For him, driving heavy armour across Salisbury Plain in no way beat the adrenalin rush of the Riphay scuffle in the Exe river valley. This is a custom, rare for its lack of apples or a hobby-horse that turns land-scape into a Deb'n border battlefield. Here was glorious mayhem with weasel patrols taking the day off. A carnage of metal and broken pistons drowned in mud, lost in smoke or engulfed in flame. A breed unto themselves, tractor boys find time to get muck in their eyes and impress the girls.

Wildlife climbs higher, digs deeper or just gets the hell out of it. Bull bars do the intended, towropes are appreciated, and wellies are a must. I had heard the worst, and the worst was true. Felix had already expressed his opinion. "They're all pikey farmers driving on LPG tanks tied on with binder twine, not wanting the tax, bombing around in scrapheaps." Unsurprisingly, Lawrence took not the blindest bit of notice of his brother. Wet weekend mud baths at Glastonbury Festival had never been as satisfying.

The thrill-seeker standing up on the back of a jeep, who had his head driven into a branch, saying he felt nothing, kind of set the standard. Boys and girls hung on for dear life. Shouts like 'How did he go straight through that?' 'The bumpers hangin' off,' 'That's gonna blow,' 'Ah, he's died,' 'Oh, moy Croist', and unintelligibles from the waggish, fuelled imagination.

Pride was in finding a naughty short-cut, greater pride was in finishing the course of slippery undulations, precipices and water hazards. Anything goes as long it's 4 x 4 and very noisy. A ragged Subaru estate car looked out of place among the trashed Range Rovers, expendable Japanese jeeps and quad bikes. A blue Land Rover with a stuffed white-feathered chicken stuck on the bonnet, for me, was best of show, narrowly beating something pink with homemade roll bars and no bonnet at all. However, a caked and battered vehicle with a vulgar number plate impressed those with cameras and camcorders. Cranes yanked the submerged from the mire. And at the day's end the cleanest thing around was the tractor tug. Success came to those that hurried slowly. Lawrence had a ball. And I, too, had to admit it was undiluted fun. Quaint Somerset could dissolve with detergent. I was in forgiving mood, even of the door denting 4 x 4 belligerence in Tesco's car park. That was before I had a reality check.

When the monotony of fast snack catcalls becomes loud, I tell Bilbo that she needs to cut back. Such is the cost of weekly food a security van might be a better option than plastic bags to carry groceries home. Indeed, these are times of change. Estate agents resort to busking and rattling tin cups.

Feeling public spirited, Chris, a 'potential buyer' builder friend, sought to buck the trend by meeting an agent to view a Taunton bungalow situated in what the agent described as a 'good neighbour-hood' where lots of the agent's family had lived for years. Chris had thought the bungalow worth a look. A minute was all it took. Emerging with a 'no sale', the agent found the axles of his new X-Trail resting on two on-end breeze blocks and the alloys wheels disap-pearing off down the street inside a white transit van. "'Ow oi larfed," recounted Chris. His compassion had limits, even less as the agent apportioned unfair blame. Beggar's understanding, I thought.

Cat language, on the other hand, I could comprehend. Like a weather-vane, Bilbo's greying tail was an appendage of clarity. A downturn was bad. Held high meant the happiness of a salmon sachet hopeful moment, all a-twitch was a warning sign not to give her rabbit, and tucked in close to her body was a sure sign of inse-curity when she gets fed minced bunny anyway.

Constant stretching hints that Bilbo is well advanced in years and sachet meals are infinitely more convenient than small moving packets that are feathered or furred. So I should have pity. Despite being allergic, I confess to being an ailurophile, a cat lover. Why? Because it's been scientifically proven that stroking a cat can lower one's blood pressure. In Wivey this is to be recommended, local politics being what they are within church porch, post office, shop, young farmers or beside sporting pitch. However, this is not an exclusive list. Join to it the allotments group, the parish maps group, the Womens' Institute, Rotary Club and Round Table, and one can begin to understand the nature of the beast. Then there is 10Radio. Councillor Eddie the editor is stoic, and holds it all together by paci-fying as best he can after a day as a Jobcentre manager.

I imagine his work is one of uniformity, during which tribal women are often the worse for wear. The females are easily recognised. Screaming at child miniatures of themselves, they congregate for the ceremony of 'signing on' sporting poodle cuts and top knots sprutted and tied with elastic bands. And, pale blue denims sheared off below the knee strain with honey-monster bulges, and pavement flopping trainers are fashion of the day. By night skirts become higher than knickers, and shoes lethal kickers.

All this to one side, Eddie's Jobcentre work place now has the jitters.

After receiving looks of compassion, Eddie explains that 'jitters' is a name given by chavs to those they dislike more intensely than hippies, though less so than goths. This troubles Eddie, as jitters are no more than average looking bewildered human beings just like he and me.

'Gryters' on the other hand, Eddie says, are helping keep morale "tickety-boo." These are 'anoraks' that can be seen standing on Bridgwater, Taunton or Castle Cary station platforms, with notepad and ballpoint in hand, recording train times. Fares fair, and amateurs knowing more than professionals is a very Somerset thing. And gryters know more about Great Western and Virgin 125s hurrying slowly than British Rail.

With such excitement abroad, local radio can be frustration's release to divisive prejudice. And starting life in 2004, 10Radio has become Wivey's air-wave phenomenon. A purveyor of gossip and an alternative voice of youth, views about hair, tattoos, and music are healthily debated. They hold on to the possibility of perhaps moving on to bigger things, like local girl Carrie Davis who went on to become BBC Radio 1's sports reader.

Carrie's Somerset roots are well known. Not long ago she was fetched to the headphones in the Beeb's London studio to lend a sympathetic ear to the trials and tribulations of a teenager. Stirred by the American music phenomenon Lady Ga-Ga's relish for using toes to play a keyboard, the trendy lass attempted the same in a Taunton music shop only to be swiftly evicted. The girl rang BBC Radio 1 to complain that Taunton "wasn't with the scene." Carrie was heard to commiserate.

These days Carrie describes herself as "blonde, bubbly, and ticklish". My daughter Ez remembers her bruised and covered in mud during five and half years of fun time with Wivey's women's rugby team. Rucks were always a laugh. So there was many a gesture of surprise when Carrie declared her dream to present 'Match of the Day'. For heavens sake, exclaimed Ez, the luxury loo roll league's got the wrong shaped ball, is soft, and over priced.

However, any local united interest in Manchester had only really been when a small group of community spirited Wivey locals read about successful community radio in that city north of Bath. Their thought to do it in rural Somerset received full support.

As a result, 10Radio was born and took ten local parishes 'by storm'. That was the rumour, anyway. Nobody seems to know the number of listeners. The figure 'five' has been mentioned by one person, while others added a nought or two, to obtain a community radio licence from Ofcom. Studio manager Anton, dapper and unassuming, is no stranger to sound studios having pushed the record button for the Rolling Stones' 'Honky Tonk Woman'.

The regular Thursday evening star turn, 'The Bantering Boys', conclude their show by picking up where they left off, in the pub. I have found a habit of tagging along and discovered that Chris, Leo and Michael, as a rule, never repeat anything twice.

One evening near closing time, as handy-man Adrian did late night DIY to a door using a chisel, bits of newspaper and cardboard, the buxom barmaid was leaning over a blackboard carefully writing out tomorrow's menu. "Took years to learn how to do that," observed Michael.

"It was a sandwich course," said Leo, as Wes, genius violinist and new kid on the block, joined us in waffle. He described encountering what he first thought to be a bollard in the middle of the road, while driving to the pub. It turned out to be a barn owl, sitting and staring. "Why didn't it want to move?" he asked.

"Probably thought, 'It's God'," I said, enjoying the sensation of my stool vibrating as the Guinness pumps were cleaned in the cellar below. Then the slam of the trap door, like the noise of a twelve bore going off, brought me to my senses.

"Absolutely." I heard Chris say. "The God of Owls has eyes as bright as headlights and a diesel driven heart."

"I'm ill," moaned Michael. "Bring me a pint." He had broken their rule, again.

Ernie is the sort of loyal listener 'The Bantering Boys' attract and loved visiting their website. One day I caught him visibly distressed about some critical opinion that the boys had received from a lady of certain age. "This is what happens when the government allows too much choice on the airwaves. Bring back the Light Programme and presenters in evening dress. That's what I say." 'Dauphine750' had posted. Ernie remembers those old penguins well, but times have moved on.

To me, he is a mischievous friend offering moral support who now hurried slower than most. Dabbling as a licensed 'radio ham', and having recently discovered camcorders and computer editing, aged ninety, Ernie is stooped, and very thin. Frailty has recently stopped him walking his old slobber-waddle spaniel in the morning. In his youth he knew spaniels as "good fish dogs," and enjoyed "a bit of sport with bucket and stick" that got him very, very mucky. Not for him the hunting of wild red deer on Exmoor. That was for the gentry, the aristocratic. Ernie leant toward the democratic by going glatt hunting on Somerset's mudflats.

The 'glatt' was what Ernie called the conger-eel, the big brother of the 'lant', or sand-eel. Hunting them consisted of wading, ankle-deep, through the mud. Huge boulders were heaved up, and the mud-whacked after the wriggling, writhing congers, while Ernie's dog rushed frantically around, scraping holes in the mud and attempting the difficult job of seizing the slippery fish. During his schooldays he learned 'off-pat' the rhyme:

'There was an old fellow of Steart,
Who went catching eels in the dirt.
When they asked " Any luck? "
"Up to eyes in the muck!"
Said that rueful old fellow of Steart.'

Sadly, Ernie rues the passing of the fun. Like the mud-horseman who leaned against the upright breast-high framework, gave a vigorous push, and went slithering along the buttery surface of the flats, the glatt-hunter has gone into extinction.

A part of Ernie's Wivey life has disappeared, too. After the war he worked as an electrician at the local sawmills that lay, as he describes, "Left, left, then down behind yonder from the town." They too have vanished, doing their bit for change and leaving Ernie lost in memory.

During the war his mates called him "Tea-Urn" because, after he drove his armoured car sloshing with French briny over the appalling sights on a Normandy beach, he made brews for anyone wearing khaki he could find alive.

His tea making passion led to him having a slight paralysis in his right arm due to pulling water from a Maastricht well later found to have had two dead German soldiers at the bottom. For the past fifty years he's ditched making tea in favour of homemade wine with outpouring fanaticism.

"Try some of this," he said, offering me a plastic medicine measure of clearish liquid poured from a small, unlabelled screw-capped bottle.

"What in heaven's name is it, Ern?"

"Orange brandy. Forty-two per cent, not bad, eh?"

'Um, syrupy. Nice.' I coughed, after the liquor had glooped down my throat.

"It's good for you,' he said, grinning happily and doing a wobble-legged jig before stabbing my shoulder with his index finger. "You know those four kids of yours?"

"'All but one are big fluttered fledglings. The other's still comfortable with small flutterings."

"Oh, but have you heard about the latest method of contra-ception."

"No."

"That's the one. Works all the time. You should have known that. I want to know more about your cat. When are you on next?"

"The radio? I think I might have blown that."

"What have you said, now?"

"Too much."

History is in the hands of those who write it and like many before me I'd got myself into trouble. A book is like that, especially if you go promoting it by 'ad libbing' live on radio. You say something, and ten minutes later somebody you might have mentioned goes into a local shop where a tuned in lady behind the counter says: "Oooooh, that Wood bloke 'on' just now didn't make you sound very nice." Such an occurrence prompted an early morning phone call, the gist of which was me being invited to "have a little chat."

The story's catalyst, Tad, a martial arts black belt, one of Williton's Poles and formerly the world's champion woodcarver, turned up with a grimace when the storm had abated. A third party's muddy boot marks had been scrubbed at. However, a stain with a taint of 'farm-yard' perfume remained on the sitting room carpet as evidence of a visitation.

"Sorry," Tad apologised, "My problem is I talk too much."

"My problem is that I write it down," I countered, our thoughts turning to the chap who had diversified from the bric-a-brac antiques trade into tiles and slates. "He was cross wasn't he, despite the truth?"

"Yes, luckily people have short memories."

Good news maybe, but on the flip side, I had suffered restless nights fearing those prone to writ-ing with the abandon of a dan-delion clock. "Trying to squash a rumour is like trying to unring a bell. Who said that?"

"Dunno," said Tad. "But it's blessed hard to unring any Wivey bell."

True, and if that was not enough, I disagreed with Tad on a point. People hereabouts seemed to have the memory of pachyderms, and they hone in on the little details. As he was about to leave, Tad had a thought, "Did I ever tell you about the time I found a first edition *Winnie the Pooh*?"

I thought it wise to give the radio a miss for a bit, and voiced this idea to Gill next door. "Oh, but people like to listen to your stories. They're interested where you live." she said.

I gave an involuntary twitch, hairdressing paranoia in my very own green rabbit sachet moment, mentally adding many a nought to the five. "They're much more interested in Bilbo," I said. "She's a cat that deserves a plaque. But I won't rush into it." I fully intended to carry on hurrying slowly, sure that Ernie would understand if I delayed my local air-wave return.

## TOTHERY
# BALLS, PENNIES & HOBBIT SHARKS

*"For, to be a stranger is naturally a very positive relation; it is a specific form of interaction."*

Georg Simmel (1858 –1918, German sociologist)

My narrow home street has gained a reputation for East European influence. Having forgiven the Czech spy Vavru Hagju for beginning his international espionage activities in Wivey when he came to visit his wife living in a local foreign workers camp, the town has become sensibly twinned with the distillery town of Nivnice in the Czech Republic's apple country. In honour of this, neighbours have bought little Czech-mates and I now live in 'Skoda Row', pronounced as in 'slow'.

Between my blue front gate and blue warped front door, a small space of paving slabs and cobbles, life carries on much as ever. The green leaves of wild strawberry and violet hang on in there, giving winter shivers under rusty flakes of fallen beech leaves. Hedgehogs tug sticky slugs and shy mice feast on bird-table scatterings. Peckal, the tame hen blackbird, implores me to break the cat-ice on the birdbath ignoring frustrated chack-a-chacks from her other half. Moss clings abundant in damp corners, and winking frogs and daddy-granfers hide under the remaining logs from Mr. Billinger's autumn load. Rural continuity, even in microcosm, is reassuring. In the wider world it is becoming harder to find, particularly in people.

Back in mid 1800s the vicar of Bishop's Hull, Wadham Pigott Williams, a bookish fellow, went to visit his Wivey friend, Mr. Capel. Something caught Wadham's interest while on the way, and he felt compelled to write it down:

"I was struck with the noble countenance of an old man who was working upon the road. Mr. Capel told me that it was not unusual to find among the people of those hills a very refined cast of features and extremely beautiful children, and expressed a belief that they were the descendants of the ancient inhabitants of the country, who had been dispossessed of their land in more fertile districts by conquerors of coarser breed."

If he wrote this today Wadham would be served with a warrant. Although justifiably proud of my own family's photo albums at the bottom of the antique chest of lop-sided drawers, I realise beauty is in the eye of the beholder. But does every parent believe it? I ask myself the question as the fag smoke of wan-faced moochers drifts from behind the graveyard wall on school mornings, and look on as little Les from two doors down, silver haired in retirement, puts on a scowl, sticks out his chest, and with the swagger of a farmer lugging buckets, goes about the dispersal of youth.

However, when push comes to shove there have been two types inhabiting the Somerset sticks for many a year, the 'country' and the 'countrified', and neither is particularly pretty. The country, have cider with a dash. The countrified, Les included, do not know about that. Other differences aren't quite as subtle.

Moustached, and resplendent in blue blazer and tie, Bugsy is country. He calls yellow tennis balls "big buttercups." "Evening, Chazzer!" he greeted me one evening. His was Wivey's loudest voice of support, and could be heard from Hinkley Point to 'Turkeyland', and from Burrow Mump to the M5's papier-maché camels. He was proud of Wivey's rugger tradition, uniquely boasting a pair of brothers of which one captained Wales and the other played for England, a long time ago mind you. The club was also second only to Bath as the oldest rugby club in Somerset. Bugsy did not enjoy Wivey being second to anyone.

That night we were in Bridgwater under floodlights, watching colts. The moon was full, round, the wrong shape for rugby. Our vicar, I thought, should have words. Not of the cloth himself, Bugsy always had them. He stood ebullient. He had received a rare and immaculate Jaguar-Daimler hearse in part exchange for mechanical services rendered toward a Taunton funeral director's black car fleet. Bugsy had declared to all without fingers in their ears that he was going to make the monster his mean machine in a garage yard already full of his eclectic Jaguars.

"There're still some old fashioned values at play," I said, half in thought. Many a sponsored shirt from Cornwall to east of Frome had done battle during the season; companies promoting the latest in technological advances and even the Royal Air Force, but the majority had ended defeated by those bearing the name of 'F. Billinger Log Supplier'.

Ellis, another of Wivey's mean machines, a farm reared, ruddy faced, rough handed prop, had by brutal beef prevented a home side player from grounding the ball for a try under the posts. It was a no contest. Between red sandstone soiled growth and that of the River Parrett's slippery silt there could never have been any other outcome. The white ball had popped from hands like a 'Granny-jump-out-of-bed' convolvulus flower pinched from its stem. Star-gazey and crumpled, the unfortunate looked as if felled by a whack from sleep inducing valerian root. Stood pointing at his opponent, Ellis's guttural chuckle of 'hurr-hurr-hurr' was distinctly audible from the touchline.

It was proving to be a good game. Gary the coach, chest as broad as a barn door with a smile to match, and Chris, the water bucket and sponge carrier and former bare fist boxer, both bounced around with glee. Dean, running the touchline with his flag slowed beside some irate home supporters, laughing "You're not getting cross with little Wivey, are you?"

Admittedly, my comment of Bridgwater being genetically impoverished since the severe loss of its men-folk in the Battle of Sedgemoor, was not particularly helpful.

The remarks prompted a "Come on, Wiv, even your spit's got muscle!" from Bugsy that woke the most dormant of seagulls.

Clicking a flashback from earlier in the day, I excused myself as my feet shifted uneasily with a call to nature. A blue portaloo had appeared in local woods where the Forestry Commission made a zzzt-zzzt of chainsaws. Gone are the days when a soul could be condoned for peeing behind a tree. Carole, a bra-less, T-shirted countrified dog-walker with a Glastonbury leaning would, however, have it differently. Her needs are basic.

"If you can actually bring yourself to go outside and pee on the ground," she had confided, "'the mineral stuff is going to mother earth. Those minerals wanna be under the ground. That's their realm. Go back through, and it's just a natural connection. Amazing, amazing. When you think about it, obviously that's what we all would have done. We wouldn't be peeing on a piece of porcelain." Wrong,

I thought. A friend has for years kept earthworm-craving badgers off his small lawn by sprinkling its edges at dusk with the contents of the previous night's chamber pot.

However, there was still more to come from Carole, "It's so much a part of the natural process to go in the woods. When I take the dogs for a walk in the woods, I always take tissues in the pocket of my Barbour. And the relief, I can't tell you. You just have to do it for yourself and then realise the complete shift in your body afterwards. I've kept meaning to share it with you. It's grounding stuff." I restrained myself from sharing that she was in all likelihood creating badger free zones. If further evidence was needed, badgers are said to keep their distance from the Glastonbury Festival site for days and nights after the Pyramid Stage falls silent.

"Absolutely, Carole," I said, remembering some pennies worth admiring. For instance, cat urine glows under a black light. And then there's the long, fallen tree trunk trimmed of its bark that's initialled 'F.H.' lying beside the River Barle half a mile upstream from Tarr Steps. The log's an art installation. Hundreds of one and two pence pieces, hammered into chiselled grooves in the grey timber, shimmer in sunlight. Pennies in the wood, indeed.

Yet, perhaps, Carole's preferences were a safer option than Dulverton's new-fangled lavatories that were branded a joke and an embarrassment after five people were locked-in in a week. Mike Gammon, a Dulverton district councillor, told colleagues on the council's cabinet committee: "I'm offering a prize to the person locked in the loos the longest." The council put up information signs in the new toilets explaining how to get out.

Shout, hoot and holler until hoarse, but if you so much as blink, modern times tickle. And as they do, unfamiliar faces replace those missed.

In Wivey, 'Horse', as his name suggests, was a huge lantern jawed man; and for years he ran the bottom bar of the White Hart Hotel. Always on hand to sort out any stool-toppling guddler, or maker of trouble, his exit line was one of the best: "You'm leavin'. Pick a window."

One man who never caused Horse any bother was thin faced, trilby-wearing Joe Hawkins. Sitting at the bar Joe would blink from behind thick-rimmed spectacles, and in his soft dialect retell again and again about unearthing a thousand Roman silver coins, now in Taunton museum, from under his plough while preparing the ground for 'tayters'.

But of Wivey's earthy characters it is probably 'Dicky Two–shovels' who is most missed. A gentle man whose real name was Richard

Vellacott mirrors a fading Somerset. During his working life he had been a farm worker with a special talent for 'taking off' lambs when it was difficult. The tools of his trade were a bucket of warm water with disinfectant, a cloth, and plenty of carbolic soap. I knew him briefly in his retirement, and asked him about challenging lambing days.

"'First," he said, "there's plenty of time. There's no hurry. That lamb took six months to grow and there's plenty of time. A lot of people get flustered up and they pull this and push that and muck everything up. Sometimes a ewe will kick and try and get up. You have to twist your leg over round the front and press it on her head. It's very awkward. Sometimes a lamb will come just by the tail. Then you have to turn the back legs around, without letting them push. You've got to get your hand inside so you can catch hold the two back legs and get those toes in your hand and bring those toes forward so they won't go through the womb. Not easy."

Small, with a face of unshaved shadow lined with the wisdom of age, he always wore tweeds decorated with half a hedge. Green-fingers replaced lambing ones, and he used to go around old people's gardens with a wheelbarrow, a brush, a pick and a shovel, never charging anything for welcome gardening work. Throughout his life acts of kindness had been borne out of childhood memory.

When he was eight years old his mother made him come home from school at dinnertime, and for that a lot of the boys gave him stick. One afternoon when Dicky returned to school, he found to his dismay that a few boys had emptied all the school inkwells over his exercise books. He never said anything and got caned by the school-teacher. When he got home in the evening, his elder sister told their mother that Dicky had been caned "fer nuffin," and his mother caned him again.

Afterwards, he believed, unfairness was part and parcel of the laws of nature. For the rest of his life bucked the trend.

Dicky Two-shovels along with Horse and Joe Hawkins and have all "gone on', and Wivey church was full for each of their funeral services.

Replacing them alongside the 'country' and 'countrified' are the 'nu'. That is to say, 'new'. It is a term that gives rise to discussions trying to identify what a 'nu' is. I give an example. Recently, as I step-ladder teetered, window cleaning, having neighbourly banter of the nonsensical sort that eases one through the chores with Gill from next door, my cat flattened herself against the street tarmac in a patch of sunlight she had discovered. A large black mongrel with grey-grizzled muzzle and lolling tongue was padding around the corner. Its owner, a wild-haired women in trackies and pumps, trotted breathlessly

31

behind, losing distance, holding a plastic bag between thumb and finger. I had never seen her about Wivey before.

"Is there a dog mess bin around here?" she wheezed. The dog had crapped a kilo.

"No," I said, and then to Gill's horror, added, "Just chuck it over the churchyard wall." She did. Oh, gawd. "Sorry," I called out, "I was joking!" With a glare she retraced her steps to retrieve the offending matter to discover the other side of the wall a grave was in the process of being dug. I could see it from the top of my ladder. The flying bag was witnessed by the gravedigger and a couple of contemplative bereaved. Looks indeed can kill.

"Nu," I said.

"Oh yes, nu," agreed Gill, "Then again with you being such a sight of special scientific interest, you are a 'nu', too. And the scruffiest at that." She had a point.

On the opposite side of the appearance scale, the smartest 'nu' are women of a certain age who come weekend knocking. They arrive in pairs, one leading a tag-along, and bear the 'Watchtower'. Immaculate beings. Powder-nosed and lipstick. Coats without fuzz bobbles. Nails manicured to gloss. And, hair set in dryer-moulds polished off with scented spray. They are walking, door tapping incen-diaries that I politely shoo away while putting outside the wood-burner's red-glow ash.

Admittedly, even before the Roman buried silver, outsiders have been discovering Wivey, but since the first road maps by John Ogilvy were published in 1675, a drip became a trickle. By the end of the eighteenth century as many travellers appeared in the town as visit the Republic of Moldova today, about two-hundred a year. A random comment, I know, but documentary film work has drawn me to Chisinau, quite regularly. And I have been there more times than to Nempnett Thrubwell.

Despite Moldovan Cyrillic printed maps making life difficult, the open-hearted hospitality of that country is touching to the point of tears. Maybe the same emotion felt by me a long way away from my warped blue font door gushed from the many characters turning up in Wivey when doled out parish money by the Elizabethan poor law.

Amongst the hundreds that once benefited from the coffers was a Dutchman, put ashore in Deb'n. Some folk of guddling persuasion, would have it that he was just a hungry soul on his way to Taunton looking for Deb'n hams. That, of course, is complete hogwash. Perhaps nearer the truth is that the Dutch love Somerset. Certainly the lowlander trail blazed the arrivals to come of summer cyclists, Spar stores, and Somerset cricket's fast bowling, Andre van Troost. The latter became nicknamed 'Trooster'. With the whimsical waggery of the boundary edge, loud crowing followed his run up to the wicket, inspiring great endeavour. In 1995, Andre bowled a bouncer to West Indies captain Jimmy Adams. It was such a whister-twister that it fractured the batsman's cheekbone. Cock-a-doodle-doo, indeed.

Lost in translation continental drift, like one of rooster's balls, gathers pace. Strange street prattling prompts local nudges in Co-op and butcher's shop, where naïvety can lead to a pickle. Recently, the young lad behind the counter in Thorne's the Butcher's was only trying to be friendly. "Danke jeun,' he said, handing pork chops and change to an accented lady. "I'm not German," she retorted loudly, clearly offended. "I am Dutch!"

The door shut with a bell tinkle and slam.

While the bewildered lad composed himself by shrugging and uttering 'Grockles' under his breath, an elderly local in the queue nodded understandingly. "It's the war. Tulips and sauerkraut don't mix," she explained. "But they both like their pork."

Dutch and Germans aside, the news of Somerset money put in pocket has reached Europe's pig slaughterers. And those from Romania and Poland flow to Wivey's abattoir to earn it. News of this gave our Somerset fairies the heebie-jeebies about bloodletting on a Tolkien scale, as they have been known as 'pigs' hereabouts for an age, whereas a weasel takes the name 'fairy'. Dialect is an added problem to both the drift and the mix.

Yet, it is the gargantuan plants of local farmer Harry Farrington that have caused the biggest stir. A jumbo sized one, that Harry calls 'diversification.' His family came to live in an extensive house that was built at a time when Wivey's Fox Brothers made blue dyed cheap woollen cloth called Penistone to attire the Empire's beleaguered slaves in itchy uniformity. Taunton carriers in those days earned themselves goodly sums of up to £6,000 a year, enough these days to pay the weekly wage of a Yeovil Town centre forward. However, from Somerset's easterly margin land, Bath born David Hartley effectively put an end to the carry on. Considered by many wet behind the ears, David was the first MP to put the case for abolition of the slave trade before the House of Commons, moving a resolution in 1776 that "the slave trade is contrary to the laws of God and the rights of men".

Slave diet, too, could be seen in the same light especially when my friend, JC, mentioned that local historian 'Deaf Derek' spoke of Porlock Weir's herons being pickled in barrels of cider to be the diet on the ships of misery.

It was an unlikely story, but not impossible. Roasted heron used to be a culinary delicacy in Somerset. A fifteenth century manuscript gives a short recipe:

"Take a heron; lete him blode. And serue him in al poyntes. in scalding, drawing, and kuttyng the bone of the nekke a-wey. Breke awey the bone fro the kne to the fote Lete the skyn be on … roste him and sause him. This sauce is to be mynced with pouder of gynger, vynegre, & mustard."

But heron on the slavers? Let it be said, JC wasn't always reliable. He himself, had a habit of only listening with half-an-ear creating the danger, given time, of rumour becoming legend. And Somerset almost had enough of those.

Better to nip things in the bud and shout at Derek, myself. I chose a day when beach pebbles were sun-warmed and tree mallow, wild fennel and sea spinach were abundant. Painted lady butterflies, bypassing immigration control, had just arrived a bit tatty from Africa to lay their eggs and flake-out on clumps of pink flowered valerian.

Now almost seventy, Derek speaks in the strong Somerset vernacular and runs the Weir's tiny 'Boat Shed' museum. The door is left open from late May allowing swallows to flit in and out, as he messes around in blue overalls, or goes fishing on his boat *Lyn Marie Two*, named after his wife who stays as number one.

With the tides right Derek took me 'dogging', and there was nothing vulgar for Lyn to worry out.

Dogfish can best be described as hobbit sharks. Grey with black spots and a white underbelly they are pretty-carnivorous. When bought with a bag of chips, dogfish are sold more appetisingly as rock salmon. They hunt the waters below Exmoor's steeply descending wooded coastline in packs. Voracious. Lying in wait in the submerged petrified forest at Gore Point for snacks of squid hook-bait. As I bided my opportunity to ask Derek about herons, many a struggling hobbit was snagged. Their skin is so rough that in the centuries before sand-paper it was used by carpenters to smooth wood. As my knuckles bled, I concocted a story, 'The Parson of Porlock', to tease local knowledge.

All the while I listened to Derek talk and kept in mind that stories can also become accented. Martin, a West Coker GP, had recently given me an appropriate example after an aged farmer had come to the surgery.

"Can you help me, doctor?"

"Hope so. What's the problem?"

"It's m'urin'."

"Well, wee into this sample bottle and I'll do some tests."

"Very good doctor, but 'ow's that goin' ta 'elp m'ears."

Beside the formidable pillar of the wave-turbine offshore from Foreland Point lighthouse, I cupped my hands and bellowed the question mimicking in Rod Hull and Emu fashion a heron's head and neck with my fingers, hand and forearm.

"Eh?" said Derek. "Urin? Yer daft nit." He put his index fingers a short distance apart in the habit of a modest fisherman. "Urrin'. URRIN'. Shoals of 'em 'ere." Derek laughed until the tears came. I felt a twit. Slaves ate Porlock Bay herring. Of course, they did.

Shamefully, the slaves were not allowed an opinion on the quality of those cidrous rollmops that probably went down as well as David Hartley's motion. And there was a further travesty. When the 'Parson of Porlock' was read aloud by local BBC radio's Lois Harbinson a lady from Chard wrote to complain that the story had made her feel liverish and spoilt her tea. JC, on the other hand, joined the RSPB.

# The Parson of Porlock

Where the grey sea cuts and gouges and the pebbles and boulders become rounded, the parson of Porlock went fossil hunting. Not that he ever found much. Children young and old would cover their mouths with hands and giggle. The joke was forever the same as the bonneted and doddery took the Sunday air to and from St. Dubricius church. The parson and his fossils. The very stuff of jest. Harmless. The parson liked his ladies.

"Morning parson, nice to see yer. Goin' on all roight?", the good natured folk of Porlock would say as he passed in the street. "Oh, tip-tapping, tip-tip-tapping", the parson would reply. Indeed everybody thereabouts knew him as Parson Tip-Tap, a gangle of eccentricity who carried stone creatures in his pockets. Creatures that clicked against a whisky filled hip-flask as Tip-Tap strolled.

God is fun, God has a sense of humour. Bless all God's creatures. This is what Tip-Tap thought as he spent his time with his small hammer and chisel beneath the miles of seacliffs between Culbone Rocks and Greenaleigh Sand. Too bad if his parishioners missed him. Such is the way with whisky and wine.

Above Greenaleigh Sand was a chapel people called Burgundy because its priest was driven to the wine bottle. Driven there by grief for the loss of his fisher-son when the Spring tide came. And driven by belief in Agh-iski the sea-fairy.

The Burgundy priest waffled on and on about the unwary vanishing. Nobody, he wittered, should venture to Gore Point. Never ever because Agh-iski was nasty.

Tip-Tap knew that grief could destroy a man. Grief could send one potty. It was madness to think that God was anything other than fun.

Yet Burgundy waffle became tavern tittle-tattle and hearth-fire yarnings. Oh yes, Agh-iski was a lady who carried her victims into the water to tear and devour them. All that remained of the poor unfortunates were their livers, washed ashore by incoming tides. There were survivors, if such people could be called that. They lived as lepers in the small community of Culbone. To merely touch Agh-iski meant taking that goat path. A leper's fate.

But of course to Tip-Tap the waffle was tosh, because God is fun. And anyway, who talked to lepers?

As a wicked March wind whipped spume and spray in Porlock Bay, Tip-Tap wrapped a scarf about his head and filled his lungs with salt-licked air. Off he set to Gore as he had done often enough before. It was his Eden. Beneath the waves was an underwater forest. Primaeval. Fossilised. Tip-Tap went there to cogitate, and of course to furtle about for the Creator's disappointments.

Fantastical things must have lived at Gore before the deluge, Tip-Tap mused. He gazed out from the doorway of the ruined cottage cut into the cliff. That sanctuary from God's elements in which Tip-Tap took his tipples. The parson had never paid any heed to the tangle of old nets and nails; or given any thought as to whose they once were. Nor had he really noticed the seaweed and driftwood that lay about the cottage floor.

As the parson looked to his Eden a lady appeared by the water's edge. The Spring tide frothed over pebbles beneath her bare feet ebbing away with dragon snores. She was clothed head to ankle in seaweed and her eyes were fixed on him.

"Agh-iski born of whisky", quipped Tip-Tap, as he sipped again from his hip-flask. He pulled a fossil of a sea-urchin out of his coat pocket and began nervously polishing it with shaking hands and scarf. God is fun.

The lady beckoned Tip-Tap to come to her. The parson became spellbound. Still clutching his fossil he stumbled from the cottage, his legs all skitter-skattle. This was no mortal woman. In an instant the parson felt his wits fragmenting. He felt the slime of seaweed about his face and the taste of salt on his lips. Tip-Tap closed his eyes and screamed out for God's protection as he blindly hurled his fossil into the sodden mass that seemed about to envelop him.

Then he was alone. There was nothing about him but the wind that chilled him to the marrow. Back up the beach Tip-Tap staggered, pebble-stumbling to his sanctuary of tipples.

With fumble-fingers Tip-Tap made a cross from splintered driftwood. Stretching upwards Tip-Tap pebble-banged a nail into the door arch mortar. From the nail he hung the cross by a piece of fishing net. But all too late.

Small wonder that the Burgundy priest had been driven to drink.

Tip-Tap never took another church service and ceased to like ladies. Agh-iski touched he took the goat path to Culbone. For the rest of his days Tip-Tap would take his turn to peer through the leper window of Culbone church. "God is fun, God is humorous, Agh-iski born of whisky", he was oft heard to ramble to his friend the fisher-son.

Porlock's parishioners missed Tip-Tap. Fewer and fewer bonnets were seen at St. Dubricius's where folk had sipped wine. Sundays became as dry as fossil dust.

The ruins of Burgundy chapel are there to be seen to this day. And beneath where the eastern edge of Yarner Wood falls away from Culbone and tumbles to the foreshore the ruined fisherman's cottage cut into the cliff remains a lonely place. Still in the mortar of the door arch is parson Tip-Tap's hastily banged nail.

# FOTHERY
# CONTINENTAL DRIFT

*"Animals are such agreeable friends – they ask no questions, they pass no criticisms."*

George Eliot (Victorian Novelist. Pseudonym of Mary Ann Evans, 1819-1880)

The walls of Wivey's 'Bear Inn', known for obvious reasons as the 'Bearin'Up', soak up the grumbles of the bibblers and guddlers. Britannia is dwindling. Not a bad thing for Porlock Bay herrings, and surely something discussed between telegraph poles by buzzard and crow going online, swaying above their chat room of arable acres.

With the Empire appearing shrunk to the fields of Somerset, the old has made way for the 'nu'. Crops of elephant grass grow higher than his sheep can trampoline, and young sozzled rugby clubbers play silly night games of going native by stripping half-naked and jumping up and down in the stuff, shouting, 'We're the Foocawey! We're the Foocawey!' I am not the one to tell them that they should grow up.

I leave it to nostalgic parents to softly hum 'Oh, What a Beautiful Morning' into their darlings' lugholes before singing "miscanthus is as high as an elephant's eye, an' it looks like it's climbin' clear up to the sky," with great gusto.

Initially introduced into Europe as an ornamental garden plant, miscanthus is a bio-mass crop originating from South East Asia. Harry claims it provides clean affordable energy, fantastic wheeze free animal bedding, and of course, cover to hide in. No kidding. You could lose a seven-foot ostrich in the jungle of stalks, let alone a roe deer, fox or pheasant.

This is a high point that raises bones of contention. North of Wivey, Somerset now mimics the Serengetti. Olivia the ostrich from Wraxall was dead, and big cat experts emerging from the shadows suggest that it might just have been one of the wild cats that, some believe, prowl areas of Somerset. Chris Hall, of 'Big Cats in Britain' told the *Guardian*, "Ostriches are no pushover and it would have been a very strong creature to try its luck with such a formidable bird."

Not wanting to put too much of a damper on the excitement, female ostriches are creatures of very little brain and easily spooked. It's more likely, say cynical folk, that Olivia was spooked by a fox and knocked herself with a bash against a fence, before literally losing her head.

Whatever the truth, some of Harry's grass might have saved her from predatory eyes.

Sadly, the grass is useless for making beer and is a far cry from the golden barley fields of Porlock vale. In a brewing town like Wivey, it just looks out of place. And, the hamlets of Pickney and Stairwell close to Kingston St. Mary had been enveloped by the miscanthus maze. During a brief road trip, only a small bungalow with walls clad in weathered wooden shingles and a few desultory back-blanketed horses stood out in brief clearings, the Quantocks lost from sight.

A few of those nags might just remember, as I do, alternative four-legged means of transport, retired ten years ago, that were horses designed by committee and the fore-plodders of our current continental drift. The Bridgwater Camel Company was the brainchild of Neil, an Over Stowey poultry farmer with a bad back. His ships of the desert at Orchard Farm became a fashionable way for feature writers from the Sunday papers to see the local countryside. Much better to get the hump than sightsee from the elevated front seat of a Range Rover. Although not quite as comfortable, it fulfilled the eccentric needs of a readership living expensive lifestyles and strolling in bland-landscaped city parks far away east of Frome.

Emitting noises half-roar, half-whimper, the camels, it had to said, were charming. An odd mixture of gentleness and haughtiness they were beasts that delighted in kicking and biting, scaring ponies and making dogs woof.

Wanting to practice before an Egypt trip, I decided to have a go at the balancing act myself and was granted a creature with breath resembling the contents a forgotten large brown recycling bin. Flopped on its tummy, wet from rain, the camel's coat smelled no better. Being astride immediately felt precarious. Similar to saying "Sit!" to a spaniel, Neil shouted "Tuch!". My camel tuched. How it tuched. Like any other, my camel was not built for sitting. However, learning that the camel, giraffe, and cat are the only animals that go forwards left feet together, then their right, my suspicions were confirmed that the Creator had a sense of humour.

All Neil's camels had names, what I called mine was unrepeatable. It felt like being aboard the *Lyn Marie Two* in a strong, but steady swell, but thinking I could cope by fairly distributing my weight was foolish. I was subjected to the camel's passion for gorse and lost my dignity.

The beach was a happier experience for both parties. With sea-breeze from Bridgwater Bay in its nostrils my camel lorded it, making the famous donkeys of Weston look like minions of insignificance. Local children acclimatised, their Christmases made all the merrier when church events offered an authentic insight into our desert religion. A mere donkey carrying Mary wearing a tea-towel headdress didn't stand a competitive chance when the lofty arrival of the Three Unwise Men just looked the part. Now those children have grown up and all the next generation looks forward to is Santa.

Relative to this, 'Bearin' Up' bibblers are mumbling into their glasses that Somerset has a history of beastly fantasia. The oldest mammal known to science, a small kangaroo, had its teeth found in a fissure near Wells, and mammoth, lion, tiger, hyena and woolly rhinoceros left their legacies in Mendip caves. I have to confess that I had personal contact with the rhino. Deep in the bowels of Taunton Museum, its skull unfortunately rolled off the table to fall bonk on the concrete floor, where it rolled some more, as I filmed for a documentary. I'm sure in life, as in death, woolly rhinos were toughies.

It's reassuring that some modern woollies have acquired necks like periscopes, a wise natural selection helping early alert. Humpless camelids have arrived in Wivey's surrounding hills despite, the green slopes of Maundown and the Brendons being a long spit from the high altiplano in Peru, Chile and Bolivia. Alpacas, hobbit versions of llamas, were in residence. Soon the warning was out to be careful when strolling over Wivey's high rich pastures. Apparently, the alpacas got diarrhoea from retaining excess water in their guts. And with an up side of their fleeces having a wide range of natural colours from white, through fawn and brown to black, the downside is that their faeces look the same.

Some places in Somerset like Bridgwater, Chard, Milverton, or Pill can offer a potted history, mostly because they made pots. On the other hand, for the past hundred years, the history offered by Wivey has been a bottled one. Myth would have it that a mere staggering together of folk under a slate town roof, no matter how small, in the company of a real ale barrel seemed to allowed the building to attain pub status. If the books are correct, it happened thirty times but with shrinkage of empirical proportions, there are now only three.

But, it is still good to know where you are. "Home", wrote Thomas Stearns Eliot, "is where one starts from. As we grow older the world becomes stranger, the pattern more complicated of dead and living." I feel I have to agree. What with continental drift and the appearance of green jacketed parking wardens and ever longer lines of tacky yellow paint, the lure of life in Somerset is coming at a cost.

Enforced change is rarely a good thing, especially if made with any degree of permanence. Like double yellows, walls can also pose a problem. They are divisive structures, both Hadrian and Qin Shi Huang knew that. Berlin was famous for having had one. And Bridgwater is now bemused. Built with care out of red brick, it's the width of the highway, over seven feet high and cuts off urbane Wembdon Road from the leafy terraces of Wembdon Rise. Has Wembdon disowned Bridgwater? Or was it vice versa?

Either way folk had a right to feel ostracised. Opinion wasn't consulted. It was a fait accompli. One young undergraduate came home from University to discover the obstruction. Mystified, and with a pint or two inside, he managed to scale it so he could get home.

By recently following an AA map I almost hit the obstruction with my car bonnet. Seeing me squint this way and that, a passing desultory dog walker said he met the puzzled and lost-looking regularly. Where did he come from? I asked. To be told, "anyone can walk around the side." Local up to date knowledge can be very useful.

Living in Wembdon, are the GP inventor of Mangold Hurling web nonsense, and his wife, a nurse who while working in a Harley Street clinic treated Bin Laden for something nasty in the time before he became infamous and who cringes as she recalls asking him, "You alrigh'?" Neither takes the wall personally, but do feel a little put out by events that they call "a load of old buggerbiddle."

Cyril, however, got the heebie-jeebies. A former Union official working in the pits of the South Wales coalfield in the days of Arthur Scargill, when Cyril's daughter became a tax exile in Switzerland, Cyril sought a career change and a move to Bridgwater. He fast tracked to become a driver of main line high-speed trains. When the feeling came to slow down, he applied for a job as a driver on the West Somerset Railway. However, it wasn't for him. Driving from home to the interview in Bishops Lydeard he knew he could never cope. Somerset roads were far too confusing.

Change has caught the bibblers unaware, like aging. Chunters about parking tickets and bus stop rigor mortis are nothing compared to the rumours of oinking sheep. The fault here definitely fell on the Romanians. Or was it the Hungarians? Drift causes merging. Mangalitzas, not to be confused with mangle-wurzels, are an ancient breed of pig hailing originally from Transylvania. They had arrived in Somerset, trotting around show grounds, oblivious to being the next best thing in quality pork. Alive, like Somerset rhinos, they, too, were covered in wool. However, their longevity might extend, if they evolved alpaca necks.

Over the other side of my mossy patio wall, Romanians, a lot of them, had responded to a pink penned 'Rooms to Let' notice on lined A4, blue tacked to the door of a house with peeling orange paint. In front of it, school kids street-perform for the landlord's security cameras that peer out from behind the glass of blown double-glazing. Urban influences, that are apparently common east of Frome, have vigorous tendrils.

To quote an overheard voice: "Nu stii niciodata de unde sare iepurele." True indeed, a 'nu' never knows from where a rabbit might jump, because opportunity, the voice was acknowledging, can be found anywhere.

I know the local entrepeneur, Mr. Jack, agreed. He was in Bucharest on business after the fall of Ceausescu. Wanting to take a present home for his kids he wandered into a shop. Wasp-waisted, bored shop assistants stood arms folded in front of empty shelves, while on the level above came the clamour of people. Intrigued, Jack climbed the stairs to investigate, to find a heavy queue for curtain rings. Having learned the lesson any ring can have a value, back in Somerset he successfully charged £5 for the mystically misted to sit in the middle of his garden fairy ring of fungi.

With patience having thinned, my wife chided me that I may have enticed our countrified Romanian neighbours here by mentioning the likes of Orastie and Brasov in a previous book, and not only that, but had said too much about Wivey. Secretly, I knew Wiveliscombers that agreed with her. And Ramona from Timisoara, the place where the anti-Ceausescu revolution began in the early 1990s, knows that the Romanian influx into deepest Somerset by those seeking a quiet life has only just begun. Not all come with butchering intent. Grockles await the services of a greater number at fast food joints, hotels and Butlins.

Such a chance though should not be wasted. I must get around sometime to leaning over the mossy wall and enquire from those that doorstep sit in dressing-gowns, spooning tomatoes from tins to mouths, about the woolly pigs.

Oh, nu, nu nu nu nu.

## FANT
# PINT POTS & SCRAPPAGE

*"The man who lets a leader prescribe his course is a wreck being towed to the scrap heap. "*

Ayn Rand (Russian-born American novelist, 1905–1982)

Evelyn Waugh thought that November could be "really most curious, snow in the morning, rain in the afternoon and thunder-storm in the evening. Apparently some American professor puts it down to the approaching end of the world by collision with some fragment of the sun."

So I am always relieved when the bonfire month dwindles away with no hint of the dramatic. I prefer instead to take simple things for granted, like a pheasant being a no-no for Mensa, a stag growing antlers and a car having headlights. If not, the world might indeed turn upside down.

I was mentioning such cultural stuff over a stable yard gate as three Alsatians pawed my chinos. "George, the Roadwater Players are putting on a pantomime called 'Dracula's Christmas'. A Pole called Tad is the Dame and it's got Frankenstein's monster in it. Are you interested? Know what I mean? I'll get you tickets, if you don't mind me filming you in the audience." I was in the process of making a short documentary about Romanians integrating into Exmoor life for the annual film festival in Moldova, a nightmare of subtitling. George Cucu had volunteered himself after reading in *West Somerset Free Press* about the film needing 'a star'.

"Okay-okay, no problemo. If it's free, I come," said George.

Completely unconnected to the Romanians over my mossy wall at home, George was from Brasov in the Carpathians, Dracula country. Now in middle age he was mucking-out, sporting his first ever pair of wellies. Green ones. He used to work 'on the tools' in the building trade 'up North' before he followed his wife to Exmoor. She had got a housekeeper's job for a Timberscombe lady known locally as 'Jodhpur Wendy'.

Between George and horses, it was love at first sight. Never having worked with the creatures before, he was soon looking after hunters, or 'rag-chasers' as they are now reluctantly known. George was a natural. Somerset, he said, felt like home. Proving that, despite my allergy to nags, George and I had something in common.

What was the key difference George had noticed between Exmoor and the Carpathians? I had to ask the question. "Ducks and scissors," he said. His mother always kept runner ducks to eat the garden slugs. Any slugs she discovered, she snipped in half with her kitchen scissors and "if slug has house on back she do not touch, because it eat eggs of slug not with house." On Exmoor, George had observed, slugs and snails are made incapable of carnage by ducking themselves in saucers of beer.

In my patio tubs, I told him, the slugs seemed tee-total and I resorted to the methods of his folk-hero Vlad the Impaler. The snails, I lobbed over the wall onto the Romanian side.

By the way George scratched horse manure into his hair, I don't think he quite understood.

Safe in the knowledge that George was 'on board' I was off to Roadwater village hall to film ambient footage of full dress rehearsal, and where the players were more concerned about pint pots than saucers. The 'Pint Pot' was annually awarded for the best Big Show on a small stage.

Down the road the Porlock Pantomime Society was putting on a challenging performance of 'Snot White'. The threat from a traditional Cinderella in Bradford-on-Tone wasn't taken seriously. This was obviously a rank outsider that lacked imagination, toadying to the annual Cinderella awards at the Westlands Sports & Social Club in Yeovil.

When I arrived, emerging out of the pitch dark into the village hall filled with wattage light, I quickly learnt stage fright was not an option in front of a painted castle backdrop. Tad had volunteered his morning hours to create a latex look-alike of Boris Karloff's iconic flat-head monster mask that even little children in the audience would be familiar with. Unfortunately, after Tad left his creation to dry, Aga heat reduced it to 'The Blob'.

Tonight the make-up girl would surely earn her sherry. The most expensive items in her armoury were Tad's £4 shocking green eyelashes. The wardrobe department was a community effort and the cast, reduced to bras, bodices and boxers, helped themselves to costume garb they considered theirs from the hanger rails. Dracula helped himself to a fag and vanished into the night. A pianist plinked her exasperation at a youth struggling to find his soprano notes, while a glitter-faced goblin with a plastic nose tied on with elastic, pretended to be a bat, swooping and sliding on floorboards, risking splinters. In a corner Frankenstein's monster held court with a company of pull-ring cider cans. The lady in charge looked cross.

Among the melee, Martin Hesp, an old colleague and now a chief hack from the *Western Morning News*, directed his photographer where to poke the lens before he began note-taking. Tad was the object of attention. I peered over his shoulder and read a jotted question. "What makes a burly 16-stone bloke dress in women's clothes, shove a bust as big as a pair of championship pumpkins down his front and apply enough make-up to create a problem at a municipal landfill?" Martin hadn't mentioned the wig of rubber snakes in his artistic exaggeration, I thought.

I decided to take my leave with a camera tape full of the weird and wonderful that George Cucu would never in a month of Sundays recognise as Transylvanian. Martin, sans notebook and a chap who never lets the truth spoil a good story, caught me the door dying to know "my angle."

Unfortunately, for reasons I shall explain, my angle never achieved its bearing. A few weeks later I made a phone call after my wife had experienced M5 misfortune from a speeding grockle and her car sat sorrowfully, an insurance write-off, outside our house.

"Is that Peter Marshall?"

"Yes," came a distant shout.

"I've got a car that needs to be taken away as scrap."

"Where are you, and when do you want it moved?"

"Oh no pressure. I'm in Wivey. In the next week or so."

"That's okay, then. I'm in Cambodia at the moment but I'm paying for this call. Ring my garage and leave your number. I'll sort things out when I get b....."

"Hello? Hello? Nothing. Zip. So, I did as told and rang Carhampton.

"Hi. Is that Peter's garage?"

"Yes."

"Whom am I talking to?"

"Peter, I'm at the top the yard."

"I thought you where in Cambodia."

"No, last I heard Peter's in Thailand."

"I've just spoken to Peter and he said he was in Cambodia."

"Then you're better informed than me. I'm Peter, too. Who're you?"

"Charles Wood."

"Is that the Charles Wood who makes films?"

"Yep."

"The same the same Charles Wood who rolled his car over in front of the Luttrell Arms front door?"

"Um, yeh. Infamy." I said.

"Infamy, infamy they've all got it infamy. Charles, it's Peter, the long-haired twiticus you used to drink with in the 'Stag'."

"Hello long-haired twiticus, how's Bish?"

"Flourishing. Bish was the first on the scene, the one who started the crowd. He thought you were better entertainment than 'Dunster by Candlelight'. And the biggest thing to hit town since Tesco's."

I thought of the Olde tea shoppes, the newsagents and the new-age crystal shop but couldn't quite place the insidious supermarket. "You what?" I said.

Peter told me I must have hibernated, and patiently explained that a Tesco TV advert was filmed in 2007 on Crown Estates-owned land using secluded areas of Croydon Hill, between Dunster and Timberscombe. There was a crew of dozens with cameras, lights and helicopters. The town was buzzing for two days. Apparently it was all in aid of a two-for-the-price-of-one clothing offer, and showed the barmaid from the Luttrell Arms riding on horseback through the woods. "Mind you," said Peter. "You went one better. You made the town buzz for at least a week, and drew more wows than the pretty barmaid, given that it was her night off."

I was oblivious to all that, but by accident, at least I had redis-covered the Bohemians, driven away when snaggle-toothed Barbara had to sell-up and Dunster pubs' character fell foul of patterned carpets and became de-snugged. Bearded, beanie-hatted, gentle Bish was apparently fine having discovered Weatherspoons where he could get four pints for the cost of Tad's lashes, and still manage to cut his consumption – the effects of a good woman.

However, my conversation with Peter alluded to why I missed the opening night of 'Dracula's Christmas'. That evening, shortly after

'Drink to Me only with Thine Eyes' chimed out from St. George's church tower, I indeed had an audience to myself after headlight failure caused me to clip an ancient stone beside the Yarn Market. Steering-rack broken, my beloved car rolled ever so slowly on its roof. To the sound of dripping diesel a hand pushed aside the airbag and the village idiot offered me 'a smoke'.

Lifted up from all fours, I was helped by the kind-hearted into the Luttrell bar for a hot cuppa. Still in shock, I thought of there being no film for Moldova, and also of Chris. His grown up children had paid for him and his wife to stay in the Luttrell's famous two-hundred-pound-plus-a-night Oak Room. This followed on from them learning that when their dad and mum married they only had £6 between themselves in the world, and the honeymoon was a wet walk around Dunster. I remembered Chris being flabbergasted at the overnight cost of the gift. His touchline words from rugby tickled me, "Oak? M'arse. 'Twas me that put in the polystyrene beams in 1976. Couldn't believe me eyes when the lorry driver passed 'em through the window. Thought 'ee must a'bin on spinach."

Remembering Chris's story must have put a smile on my face. "What's so funny," said a policeman.

"Nothing." Given where I was, I thought it was best to keep a confidence.

The news of my carnage though was soon out. Two minutes for it to be around the village, twenty for it to be across the Somerset. Bob, the County archaeologist, had heard on the radio as he finished work that the Dunster road was closed. "Another, festive drunk," he owned up to thinking, braking his bicycle to chat, sporting one of those furry Russian hat with ears flaps that made him look like a playful puppy. "Didn't know it was you."

The initial reaction of Steven, my publishing editor, was to put on his Member of the Park Committee hat, and hope the stone was undamaged. I kept it to myself for a bit that there was blood on the book contract lying unsigned on my front passenger seat at the time. 'Surviving another Somerset Year' seemed ironic. My car, though. was a goner and with it the foibles and eccentricities.

At least young Sam Jeffs might benefit. In his early twenties and known because of his rasta hair as the 'dredded sculptor', and a pretty hippy who 'does' the festivals, he had a ruthless streak when it came to departed mechanical friends claiming "cars are like women – it takes years until you think you understand them and then it turns out you still never do." Sam lives off the radar down a rutted Willett track in a customised ancient Dodge truck with portholes and a steel door.

Outside, a rabbit invariably hangs on washing line. He is not a daylight fan but by night the dark is illuminated with sparks as he welds his creations of scrap out of car jacks and spark plugs, sheet metal and drive shafts that fetch thousands in London. The donation of my little green wreck was gratefully received. Once transformed, I would never be able to afford to buy it back.

Quite a galling thought.

Eventually, Peter Marshall turned up in his scrap lorry complete with chains and an hydraulic arm. Soon my wife's car too was being lifted to doom. As Peter let his Alsatian-cross take a piddle in Wivey school car park he broke the tension relating a conversation he'd had with a farmer.

"You're a bit handy with that thing," the farmer said.

"It's all the playtime I have."

"Try and get your links over that tap," the farmer challenged, pointing at the corner of the farmyard.

"No, prob." And it wasn't, not with a deft touch on the buttons and levers. To say the farmer was laughing was stating the obvious. Sadly, Peter was a little too keen on the release and managed to rip the tap and pipework out of the ground hurling it with velocity through the farmer's barn roof.

"Now, I'm cryin'," the farmer told Peter.

"Boys toys," I said.

Having a laugh himself, he took a wad of notes as big as a score of ponies from his pocket and peeled off a tenner. "Happy days," he said.

After Peter disappeared Jeremy from next door knocked on the warped blue front door. He had been doing his re-cycling duty and found tea-stained copy of the *Western Morning News*. "Do you want to keep this," he asked, "You're in it."

Martin had written his article, two lines of which read, "The night the WMN paid its visit the Players were being filmed by a Westcountry documentary maker called Charles Wood, who is putting together a programme for Bulgarian TV."

Never believe everything in the press.

Ironically, the pantomime was not yet over. Fate still had a part to play. My car carnage proved an irrelevancy. The Moldova film festival had to be cancelled. The youth of Chisinau had taken to the streets protesting at the Communist election victory based, it was claimed, "on the votes of 400,000 dead Romanians." The atmosphere was not convivial for an international gathering with tanks rumbling about. George Cucu spending Christmas with Dracula on Exmoor would never have received the attention deserved. And the awards? Well, the Bradford Players took the Pint Pot and 'Snot White' swept the rest. For the Roadwater Players and myself there would always be the hope of another year. At least I was spared the subtitling.

## SAHN
# BUGS & BIM-BOMS

*"Delusions of grandeur make me feel a lot better about myself."*

Lily Tomlin (American actress and comedian)

The weather had turned icy, garden molehills were solid lumps and the cockcrow from across Wivey's churchyard sounded mournful.

"Ez, did you know a cock's comb can drop in heavy frost?" I asked.

"That's sick. By the way, so's the cat. She caught a rat. And she's scratching again."

With elephant grass rustling brittle brown, Christmas season was in full swing, England shut, and my daughter Ez was dressed like a hobbit. Puffy top, knee length trousers, floppy suede hand-made shoes and in between them calves brown with the tan of a year's backpacking in Australia, she and her friend Charlotte had returned from long weekend in Dublin. They had a shared opinion that Wivey parish church was 'a damned sight more impressive' than the cathedral beside the Liffey. As it was not fashionable to ask whether Wivey had delusions of grandeur, Ez put the question to me another way. "Why was Wivey so up itself?"

"History," I said, "Cause and effect." Ez got the glazed look of disinterest she reserves for any irrelevancy over a week old. Used to it, I wasn't deterred. "Want to hear about the bishop and the fleas?"

"Go on, then, if you have to."

51

I told her that it was all the fault of Bristol. During the mid-1300s, ports throughout the rest of Europe knew better than to allow brigs of disaster to land dubious cargos stored in their gunwales. The Bristol merchants, however, were irresponsibly greedy. From off the ships though came not only Oriental goodies, but horrible symptoms of shivering, blood-spitting and blackening glands. Somerset was one of the counties worst affected by the 'Black Death'.

Writing from across the county at Montacute in Edwardian times, Llewelyn Powys noted that, "there was no more care for dying folk than men would care nowadays for goats. Scarcely would the death-bell cease from tolling for one departing soul than it would boom out again for another. The cattle wandered free, the corn was left unharvested and the young man who made merry with an unexpected legacy on Monday, lay mute in the churchyard's yellow clay by the time the sacring-bell of St. Catherine's was heard to tinkle on the following Sunday. Throughout our scattered villages and homesteads the wretched labourers and poor folks, with their families died by the roadside, or among their crops or in the cottages."

Wishing to avoid a sudden demise themselves, the wealthy did a runner. Among them was the Bishop of Bath and Wells, a godly chap called Ralph Shrewsbury. Prudently avoiding the more populous districts of his diocese, he quickly retired to his manor house in Wivey that had been refurbished for a lengthy stay, including the erection of a personal chapel. Suffering an understandable drop-off in clergy, Ralph came up with a solution, confirmed by papal indulgence in March, 1349, that proved too much knowledge is a dangerous thing. Parishioners could choose their confessor in their hour of death. Even a woman would do, if a man wasn't available. Perhaps this was the precursor to guddlers telling their life stories to the barmaid in the 'Bearin' Up' before facing the music at home, a befuddled soap-opera weekly re-enacted in every Somerset corner.

These days only the red sandstone gatehouse remains. Of the Bishop's palace there is nothing. The end came after it was turned into a workhouse. Wivey folk pilfered the building away stone by stone, deciding on better uses for it, like putting their own houses in order, including a newer and bigger church. Many agreed the old one was piddly. A crack in the tower from a lightening bolt was a Godsend, giving reason enough to reach for sledgehammers and commission the grand design of the popular Taunton architect, Richard Carver. He was man with a penchant for churches, country houses and spending money.

In 1829 a new St. Andrew's rose from among the crocuses, it's exterior stonework covered in render that some wanted whitewashed like at Selworthy and Withycombe. The latter being famous for its long-haired man wearing a hat. Hidden in a wall recess of St. Nicholas is one of the earliest church monuments to include such headwear. The figure carries a heartcase meaning he died elsewhere and only his heart was brought to Withycombe for burial.

New St. Andrew's had no such treasure. But was it an edifice fit for a bishop if he ever fancied a visit? No. Much better to knock the render off. It would make the new church 'more in keeping' with whimsical Wivey. The irritation caused by render was on a par with the loss of the valuable Norman font. It, too, vanished to be rediscovered years later, an imposing birdbath suitable for buzzard ablutions in a churchwarden's garden.

In the meantime, something of note was needed. Eventually, a war memorial apse was plumped for, and it was to be designed by a capable hand that wasn't overly busy. Renowned for his work at Glastonbury, Frederick Bligh Bond, known to his friends as 'Bligh' and a chap who had unearthed a Saxon cross used to inspire his design for that town's war memorial, was the contentious choice. He was a tie-wearing, smart dresser and had the receding hairline and glasses of a scholar. His CV was impressive, 'Fellow of the Royal Institute of British Architects and a member of the Somersetshire Archaeological and Natural History Society' a great-grand nephew of Captain William Bligh of Bounty infamy, and in 1908 the first person to conduct a meticulous archaeological dig of the ruined Abbey. The work was unpaid and seasonal, a charitable gesture. It was his discoveries that started the notion of King Arthur's grave and a mystical visit from Joseph of Arimathea to Glastonbury. Then ten years later he made the mistake of writing a book, *The Gates of Remembrance*, about discovering the Abbey's Edgar Chapel that, to the Church of England's consternation, revealed him as a mystical mystic. Through a medium, a Captain J. A. Bartlett, and a pencil Bligh had had the help of long-dead monks by means of automatic writing.

"Can you tell us anything about Glastonbury," Bligh had asked an unseen communicator, or, as he apparently then understood it, the universe. In clear, eloquent English, the answer came back: "All knowledge is eternal and is available to mental sympathy." After a short interval, more words flowed: "I was not in sympathy with monks – I cannot find a monk yet." Further sittings resulted in a hotch-potch of communication, some in English, some in Latin, some in monk Latin, a combination of Old English and Latin. Some were signed, others were not. One Johannes Bryant emerged as the chief communicator, speaking in monk Latin, but there was often a change of influence making it unclear whom the communicator was. As a group, the communicators referred to themselves as "The Watchers."

Bligh found cause to wax lyrical: "Give it truth to feed upon and it will evolve truth. And through the door of truth may enter that which will guide us to a wider knowledge."

Understandably, Dorothy L. Sayers described Bligh as " the oddest little gentleman." She wrote, "He sits and talks about spirituality, archaeology, the fourth dimension and the mathematical relation of form to colour, till you don't know if you are on your head or your heels". Francis Thyer, Deputy Custodian at Glastonbury Abbey, says Bligh is a father of modern archaeology. Obviously, Wivey had found itself a small treasure.

Then came Wivey rumours of other valuables after a grockle who listened to the BBC Radio 4's Making History, wrote in to the programme. In her nosiness, she had been flabbergasted to unearth war records of a small group of people squirreling away important examples of church stained glass and artifacts from all over the country. Who was behind this? Why Wivey?

The programmers discovered that the plan to move hundreds of objects of church art, furniture and relics was that of another grockle, Dr Francis Eeles, a bigwig in the Central Council for the Care of Churches. Wivey was chosen for his own convenience. He had a holiday home in Dunster. Practically speaking, however, the church did have a huge crypt neatly divided up into small vacant sections. The crypt was purposefully designed that way to help pay for the building. The idea was that the Wivey worthies would pay rent for a place where family members could be buried. This genius idea never really worked and much of the space was just that, space. In the early months of the war Francis changed that. Ever since, due to its size and content Wivey church might be forgiven for having delusions of grandeur. Not so the bim-boms. Despite their noisy boasting they can't compete on weight.

While Wells Cathedral, famous for banging out tunes like 'Kent Treble Bob Royal' has the heaviest ring of ten bells in the country with a tenor called 'Harewell' weighing over 56 cwt, Queens Camel has one of the heaviest rings of six, and East Pennard the heaviest five. The treble at East Pennard is the heaviest in the world, weighing over 11 cwt. Trying to keep up, Bishops Lydeard church tower has suffered bell motion damage. The call to service sets the tower swaying in a way that can be felt in the upstairs ringing-room, making folk feel almost 'sea-sick'.

In Wivey, it was not just about feelings of heaviness. The ringers struggled with tunefulness. This had prompted another question to be asked. Who was the subversive that had pinned a note to the church tower door requesting that the campanologists 'peel oranges rather than our bells'? Quite rightly, the educated guess was someone incapable of spelling 'peal' correctly, sparking chunters of local schooling failures.

At which point, Ez, although seeming not to have been listening to any of my ramble, absorbed as she was in a box of dates, suddenly perked up. "I heard about that in the pub. Nobody's admitting it." She sniggered as the bim-boms announced the imminence of Midnight Mass. Surely Scouse Graham, the vicar, could pray for enlightenment to fertle the culprit out. But no, he was leaving. What a shock, so much so the news had made the local paper. Yet more change. Two and half thousand jaws had dropped. Owls, squirrels and pigeons became anxious.

After fifteen Wivey years Scouse Graham was almost a local; part of the scenery he helped to preserve. He was a hero with power that showed itself when a 'grumble-patch' churchwarden had wanted to chop down the cemetery's great copper beech tree, home to squirrel and owl, for not being 'in keeping'. And because it provided lofty lookout perches for condor sized pigeons eyeing his allotment's winter cabbages. Graham simply wagged a finger and air was filled with coos of gratitude, cheerful chitters and moonlight hoots.

Yet the shrieking gull atop the church weathervane was a constant reminder to the Liverpudlian rector of his twenty naval years at sea before his calling. To escape further inland would surely be refreshing.

Many in the 'Bearin' Up', however, believed that missionary zeal had been the reason for Graham accepting Frome. He was to become the moral protector of thirty thousand from the niggling pagan lands to the east, even if only a fraction of that number ever passed through God's portal.

In the seventeenth century people had to go to church. Parliament said so. But more and more there was reluctance for neighbours to snitch on one another. Churchwardens and sidesmen of Wivey found themselves in trouble with the authorities for not reporting absentees from church to a justice of the peace. And there was absenteeism enough, as there usually was in such clothing towns and villages. At least twenty Wivey Quakers did not attend Holy Communion, including the town's plod and bailiff.

That Christmas Eve there was flu about, but to quote Garrison Keillor, the American humourist, 'A lovely thing about Christmas is that it's compulsory, like a thunderstorm, and we all go through it together.' The imminent dog-collared departure meant the church was bulging at the seams. Perhaps God was a dog person, I thought, fair reason why the only domestic animal not mentioned in the Bible is the cat. Having given Bilbo a consoling pat, my wife and I joined the throng, hoping to meet up with Felix, my youngest. Instead, he was trapped, as he later explained, making ten-inch roll-ups in the pub and unable to circumnavigate a very large lady in purple leggings, her grey hair in bunches framing a face that looked as if a thousand cigarettes had been stubbed out on it.

Reg, the elder statesman of the pump attendants from Jones' Garage personified sobriety as he reverently read the lesson, to the astonishment of many who had earlier witnessed him attempting a dishevelled moonwalk in the rugby club bar.

Speaking via microphone distortion, Scouse Graham then gave a sermon about journeys. Lit by spotlight from up on high like the angel Gabriel, he made a pregnant pause when red-faced latecomers, prised out of the 'Bearin' Up', made a cringing entrance.

They exchanged quizzical glances as pulpit words spoke of congested roads and roundabouts, red streams of snail pace tail-lights in the dimpsey dark, and that all-important last minute present being an elusive thing. Had it been easier for the Three Wise Men to find gold, frankincense and myrrh without resorting to Debenhams, the County Stores, and the Pawnbrokers? Searching questions. Awkward. Eyes rolled to the ceiling and the white patch up on the nave's vaulted purple roof. How to paint it? Did tall folk develop a stoop due to low cottage ceilings? Distracting stuff.

Then the coughing began. So did the head shaking and whispers.

Unrest began to spread. At the time of blessings between one and all, it became epidemic. By the lessons learnt from Ralph Shaftesbury, one's neighbour was a hazard, a latched pew a possible sanctuary. Folk, in pews behind and in front, courteously tried to be ignored. Handshakes were done nervously wearing a glove. The words, 'May God be with you,' were a mumble, trusting to luck.

But, oh horror, it was to no avail. Naïve twits, caught up in the spirit of Christmas, lifted their pew latches and went abroad spreading goodwill and a fortnight of sneezes and misery to those too polite to refuse them.

Those that escaped came a cropper with the chalice of communion wine. Heavens, the sidesman wasn't wiping the rim between sippers. Beside me, Mike Thorne the multi-award winning Wivey butcher received the Lord's blessing, though undoubtedly not a turkey's, as a stage whisper erupted from a rattled rail kneeler further down the line, "For God's sake, man, use your cloth on the bloody thing." This was perhaps the very reason the Bishops of Bath and Wells had called for a private chapel. No need to mix with the commonalities, and less risk of catching something contagious.

As we of the congregation finally scuffled toward the church door and a final shake of the vicar's hand, one of the latecomers, long-haired and sans hat, wished me well and thought my previous book "quite good." Then telling me to move on, he kissed an astonished overcoated man behind me. I wondered what deserving joy was left unrequited that happy morning.

Behind the warped blue front door, Bilbo was scratching herself again, so I squeezed her Christmas present, a capsule of liquid de-fleaer, in the 'un-get-at-able' spot at the back of her neck. If only it had been available for rats, I thought, before feeling a little dizzy.

## DAHNY
# PENDULOUS NUTS & MUDDY-WANTS

*"It is no use asking me or anyone else how to dig. Better to go and watch a man digging, and then take a spade and try to do it."*

Gertrude Jekyll (garden designer, writer, and artist 1843-1932)

I had made a film for my friend Andrew Tresidder, a Chard GP, about making flower essences like daisy brandy and scleranthus vodka that was featured in the *Mail on Sunday* magazine. It was picked up by ITV. Now Westcountry news wanted to do their own feature with Andrew on the topic of 'Ways to be Cheerful.' Should he do it? He got his answer from a pendulum, and did. I was intrigued at the thought of a doctor dowsing.

It could have consequences. And was not something confined to mystical mists. Barbara Brennan, an leading atmospheric physicist who used to work for Nasa as a research scientist, dowses with a pendulum of beech.

"You can't fool the pendulum," said Andrew earnestly. "Some people think there is a greater intelligence in the universe than we as individual egos can touch onto. And it's thought that dowsing taps into this. Whether it's subconscious or tapping into something greater we can only guess. Dowsing was very popular in Cornwall in the middle ages when it made people a lot of money by finding the right place to dig for tin, and the right place to mine. And it's been used down the ages to find water as well using hazel twigs or forked rods, and of course, the pendulum. It got a bad name in some ways because the words dowsers use, 'to divine', gets confused with the word 'divination' which the Bible doesn't like."

As far as Andrew was concerned it's a faculty that many people possess to tap into, a sixth sense side of us that we don't normally learn, because we're too busy learning maths, geography and French. I kept my silence that these had always slipped my first, second, third, fourth, and fifth senses, let alone worrying anything to do with the sixth.

Soon afterwards I discovered dowsing was endemic. Gary, a digger driver, by his own admission used two hazel sticks and confided the peculiar fact that many plant users are dowsers. Seriously. The reason? It's expensive to go through water, but dangerous to go through electricity. He admits to having dowsed a straight, forty-feet wide energy line connecting Axminster and Glastonbury Tor that passes through the churches of Dowlish Wake and Kingstone, Burrow Hill, Wells Cathedral and Mendip Aerial.

Obviously, Gary had his critics, so there was a need for a trial before Somerset ennui set in. I just had to query where Gary's got his energy from, but couldn't make my mind up on the way forward. Should I do this, or should I do that? Fiddlesticks. The radio decided matters. The on-line Taunton witterers from BBC Somerset Sound were supposed to be commentating on County Ground run getting. But no. Instead I got Bob Dylan's 'Lay Lady Lay' followed by Maggie Reilly warbling 'Away Wi' the Faeries'. A clue why this was came with the announcement: "Phil Tufnell is trying to get back into the commentary box but has been locked out." Believing there's no such thing as coincidence, I took notice of the song titles, and headed for the Blackdown ridge. Sticks other than cricket stumps must have a social benefit.

It was time to be educated, something which I felt a natural resistance to having had an old-fashioned schooling in grim institutions where bullies were lords. My fear was that I would go red-faced with embarrassment when I popped my friend Jonathan the question, "Can you teach me to dowse?"

Jonathan and Maria Farey run a small thirty-acre farm, as it would have been worked a hundred years ago – organically. As a family they don't crave money, preferring instead simplicity and nature's humour. On seeing me rattle the gate, Maria apologised for the clutter that filled a farmyard appearing much lighter than I remembered. Something was missing. Oh gawd, the barn.

Ten tons of winter snow had collapsed the extensive corrugated-iron barn roof. Jonathan was underneath at the time and his left arm still bore the bruises. A black fluffy bog-brush-tailed mog miaowed about his ankles.

"I had more lives than this cat," confessed Jonathan, taking a time-out with his guitar to strum 'Little Donkey' to 'Starlight' their children's white self-cleaning pony that looked in a state of bliss. I didn't want to disturb.

Both Jonathan and Maria said they had been tut-tidying. To me Folly Farmyard looked like normal. There was straw on the driver's seat of a rusty and flat-tyred campervan. Being kept out of trouble, 'Houdini' the Jack Russell had the passenger seat and pawed the window. One end of a washing line was tied to the top of the camper-van, the other was attached to the tool-shed. And in between hung the laundry. Pet rabbits hopped about cages, and bicycles and skate-board leant against iron-bar gates. Jonathan's first car, a 1956 beige Ford Popular with old fashioned vacuum wipers attached above the windscreen, mouldered beside 'Tigger', a snoozing old arthritic lurcher and three green Morris Minor bonnets, that Jonathan declared, had proved themselves to be "magnificent toboggans." However, a dilapidated caravan, a thoughtful gift from friends for which spiders were grateful, was to go.

As a family, the Farey's are well-spoken and admit to being "a bit alternative." Soot from the Rayburn is collected and put on the roses after spring-cleaning. Scrunched newspaper is used occasionally to clean the windows, and the furry insides of broad bean skins were used seasonally to polish shoe toecaps and bits of household china. The concession for their daughters, Jemima, Otterly, Polly and Lily, was an old, dusty and slow PC. Such a luxury had to be paid for as well as making ends meet. A regular income seemed a good idea. After drawing straws, Maria got the short one.

Jonathan got the ancient tractor and the animal husbandry. His job included hedge-laying and pandering to the needs of Hairy John, the shaggy blind Highland steer that liked best, depending on the weather, to either sunbathe or shelter under a gnarled crab apple tree. Other apple trees on the farm were Jonathan's preserve. Beneath the tendrils of last year's nasturtiums clinging to the porch roof, the tap of a large brown plastic barrel dripped homemade cidrous ooze. Jonathan liked his cider, particularly pan heated with cinnamon sticks and fresh ginger to warm the cockles of his heart.

A Gloucester import like the Old Spots pigs, Jonathan spent his formative years living off Old Holborn tobacco roll-ups and Ambrosia tinned rice, not forgetting sausages coated with marmalade and mustard. All this has held him in good stead for debate.

As a school liaison governor for the Arts at Chard's Holyrood School, Jonathan heard that a wayward teenage lad had asked about ferreting in the school library. Realising this was not a general desire to book-worm but a murderous intent toward bunnies the librarian did not think the query politically correct. And her colleagues agreed. Jonathan, somehow managed to keep his cool, recalling his father's reminiscences of following the otter hounds. These lovely dogs used to ply their trade until after the war, as fish stocks became depleted due to otter numbers. Life is all about balance. Small wonder, Jonathan argued, information at the very least should be made available to pupils on the blood sport wrangle. Better, he said, to pit your wits in nature than stacking shelves at the local supermarket.

It was an opinion shared by Andy West who had given up the job of a supermarket manager to take up traps and officially become Britain's top mole catcher in 2009. Not for him the cute, folksy Somerset names for a mole and its tunnel of muddy-want and wontwiggle. He was serious. His was a war of attrition based on the knowledge that pickle juice, broken glass, red pepper, razor blades, bleach, moth balls, rose branches, human hair balls, vibrators, ultrasonic contraptions, gasoline and explosives, don't work. This was a true professional. By trapping 690 muddy-wants in a month, news of Andy's success was of low profile achievement.

There was a likelihood that he would have got on well with Angela, Jonathan's mum, a woman of strong disposition who speared moles with a blacksmith sharpened gardening fork in the community hall garden. Certainly, on the surface, Jonathan could do with help, but instead of ringing Andy, he gets it from Richard, a neighbouring farmer of gathering years and gentle manner that revered both moles and earthworms as "the ploughs of the earth."

As Jonathan played his guitar, Richard was up in Folly's worm-rich fields with a spade and heavy duty plastic sacks bagging-up to take home the fine tilth of molehills on the back of his tractor for his wife to put on their very large garden. He did it regularly. The muddy-wants themselves, he left alone. There was no need for unnecessary suffering. Priding himself on never having harmed an animal in his life, Richard was aware of moles being haemophiliac. As he says, "to nick 'em is to kill 'em."

Like Richard, Maria is Blackdowns and has the local habit of 'making do'. She got it from her mother who as a child never had any dolls to play with, so used to lay dead rabbits down in an old pram, cover them in a blanket, and push them around. Now home to a broody hen, the pram remains a Folly feature.

These days Maria is a primary teacher at the village school in Combe St Nicholas. To look at her, never could the name 'Farey' be more appropriate. She is positively elfin.

From a string around her neck hangs an ammonite, a sort of prehistoric shellfish. Jonathan found it when he was repairing a gatepost for Hairy John's field. It was petrified in rock crystal instead of being in the usual sandstone. Jonathan cut it open with a dinosaw, she laughs.

A lady in Boscastle cave said the fossil had healing powers turning negative into positive, ideal for coping with 'bouts of domestos', so Maria has worn it ever since. Did she know of the legend of St Keyne, the daughter of a 6th century prince of Wales, turning venomous snakes into stone at a time Somerset was infested with them? Or that Keynsham was named after the saint because folk believed the ammonites, so common in the area, were the snakes of legend. I didn't ask. What I knew was that as long as I've known them, Jonathan and Maria had seemed the picture of harmony. I considered visiting Kilve with a small hammer to tap out cheap birthday presents from the rocks for a long-suffering folk I knew.

When Maria told the children in her class that her fossil was millions of years old, she said, "you could have heard a pin drop." On adding that a T Rex might have looked at it, the silence was broken by 'oohs' of wonderment.

Learning the four 'R's at Combe St Nicholas has become a family tradition. Maria's grandfather, Ken, went there, as did her mother, and now Maria's own daughters' schooldays are spent in the little school beside the church. All four generations vouch for the school being better than in the past.

Way back, a parishioners meeting, known as the 'vestry', met monthly in a church room. It appointed the parish officers like churchwardens, overseers, way-wardens, and the sexton, as well as caring for the church, highways and poorhouse. In 1748, the vestry turned its attention to educating the poor. The recorder of the overseers accounts put quill to paper to say the school-master was to be given yearly salary of twenty shillings to teach 'four poor children to read or two write'. He could also have put himself forward for spelling lessons.

However, James Thorne, the school-master mentioned, didn't take well to his new responsibility. Within a few years he was given "a Quarter of a year … to settle his affairs within the Parish, and at the end of the of the said Quarter of a year he is to quit the school unless his behaviour shall be such as be approved of by the Majority of the

Parishioners present at the end of the time, and to undertake no Deputy office for the future."

No-one is above being told off, and with James it had the right effect. Mending his ways he was still welding a cane or chucking chalk at unfortunates, even if not correcting spelling slates, eight years later.

And there's more. In the days before Council Tax and the Somerset Highways Department, parishioners were still liable for personal service to upkeep the roads in reasonable repair as an when way-wardens called upon them. For a fee, individuals could excuse themselves of this irritation. A day labourer would have to fork out three shillings a year, and double that if he was a bloke with a horse.

Owning a plough was a real problem. A hefty one-pound-ten had to be paid to avoid filling in potholes. Anyone who'd rather put their feet up was hassled and means-tested.

In 1752 it was ordered that the Constable should make an inventory of all belongings of folk who the parish relieved from local duties. One stands out.

"May ye 3, 1752. A count of Eliz. pons goods a bed and hedsted bolster on blancked and cwilt a bras crock bras skilot a cobard a tabell bord 2 barrelles a Sidbord a Braik 2 back croocks a setell to Puter Dishes a small kitell a shit."

Such language. Did James Thorne, take his job seriously? He certainly seems deserving of the vestry's slap on the wrist. The demise of English in Somerset didn't just start with the mobile texting phenomenon that gets Maria's giddy goat.

"Charles, come and see the chicken with crop burn. Poor thing's asleep by the stove," said Maria. I raised my eyebrows and was led to a hen with cotton thread stitches in its neck squatting sorrowfully in a cardboard box beside the Rayburn. The hen had escaped into Starlight's field to glut on lush grass. The crop burn was not caused by the obvious but a problem of fermentation. Maria and Jonathan administered the first aid. After Jonathan anaesthetised the bird by pouring apple brandy down its throat, Maria made a small cut in the crop's thin skin with a 'knit-unpick' and pinched out the grass. before darning the wound with needle and thread.

"She'll be and about tomorrow, right as rain" said Jonathan, who had joined us. The hen opened an eye as if in disbelief of Farey magic. I saw a window of opportunity and jumped through it.

"Jonathan, can you explain dowsing? Can you teach me to do it?" I asked, without a hint of embarrassment. I too, was under the spell.

Putting on his thoughtful expression, he said, "How do you explain the force of nature? Some people would explain it by saying that when somebody says to us, 'of course you can' we feel relaxed. And when somebody says to us, 'no, you can't,' we tend to feel a bit tenser. And, our bodies know intuitively the difference between tension and relaxation and between something that feels comfortable and not so comfortable. It seems instinctively, maybe subconsciously, we often know the answer to answers we can't know with our rational mind. And dowsers would say, when they are dowsing, that they are connecting with a greater source of wisdom than that which is just confined within our own skulls. There's something a bit more going on that we are connecting with."

Going to a kitchen drawer Jonathan took out a rusty nut tied to a piece of string. It had been a nut picked randomly from his dad's old toolbox. "My pendulum," he said.

Holding it up by the loose end of string, he asked the 'pendulum' to "show me a 'yes'."

Lo and behold it began to swing round-and-round, giving an answer quite positively. Then he asked, "show me a 'no'." the nut began swinging backwards-and-forwards. The difference in motion was clear. Yet Jonathan could probably feel my continued unspoken cynicism.

"When I did this for the first time," he said, " I held my hand as still as I could possibly hold it, and when it started moving round-and-round I thought, 'this is wonderful' because I knew it wasn't me doing it. Having seen people dowse, at first I was somewhat sceptical. I could see their arm going round-and-round or side-to-side. So I thought I'd see for myself."

He poked his chest with an index finger. "You know yourself. You know. And round-and-round it went. I knew in my heart-of-hearts there was no way of me physically having anything to do with it. This was another energy, another force. And I thought 'this is fantastic, I'm on to something here'. Now I can just think, 'show me a yes, please'. I don't even have to say it, just think it in my mind. It's wonderful the uses you can put it to. But how do we explain the force of nature?"

To me it had become obvious, ever since a small child I've known that 'please' is a magic word.

On the table were a pile of Maria's flapjacks, "Are these safe to eat?" was a fair enough, question perhaps deserving of a 'yes'. But would "Are these inedible?" also give a 'yes'?

Jonathan's answer was as clear as mud. "With both the yes and the no you are still asking for a positive answer because you are looking to protect yourself. So, something out there knows something more than me and my arm, and my consciousness. Something is telling me something I don't already know in my being. So is there an external force at work that's not accessible by our conscious mind making us use our unconscious mind? So, you can understand why people might be sceptical. They might think, "Oh, it's a lot of old baloney'. Look, hold the pendulum. You hold your hand still and you try it. Give it a go."

Well, there was no going back. With a rumble in my tummy I took the nut and asked for a sign to say 'yes' the flapjacks were safe. The pendulum went round-and-round. I was aghast.

"There you are," cried Jonathan. You've done that!" I felt the instrument of something questionable.  This, I suppose, is how everybody starts.

"Heavens," I said.

As I took my leave, Maria hugged me in gratitude for depleting the flapjacks and Jonathan mounted his old tractor that in such cash-strapped times was irreplaceable. After many a cough it started, albeit reluctantly. And with a hay bale stuck on its backside it was off. Through the cloud of smoke I could see Jonathan waving, away to feed the cattle and of course, Hairy John. Were the Fareys' happy? A nut would now be able to tell me.

# DOWNY
# SLAG & CANTICLE

*"I would much prefer to be a judge than a coal miner because of the absence of falling coal."*

Peter Cook (Actor and Comedian, 1937-1995)

The city of Bath was built from limestone mined at Combe Down. When those mines closed about the time Queen Victoria died a legacy of over eight-and-a-half miles of tunnels were left as a memory that have been filled in with aerated concrete. It's easy to forget that men also nibbled at Somerset's black heart like a series of biopsies, and I wanted a peek.

A small group of roe deer across a field gave my car the distant eyeball. Were they the guilty ones? Beasts meeting their description were being blamed for eating wreaths laid at local cemeteries. Indeed, the family of one man buried the previous week thought thieves had stolen the £500 of flowers laid in his memory. Bath and North East Somerset Council said they would be "writing to local florists with advice." The mind boggles. I look forward to the tributes of gorse.

To be fair to the deer there wasn't much in the way of exciting salad about. However, in a world of bare hedgerows and leafless trees I didn't imagine getting lost. Pootling around the east end of the Mendips I knew I was somewhere near Stratton-on-the-Fosse. Or was it Frome? My meanderings in the Chew valley between Bath and Wells had become a tad haphazard as crossroads and T-junctions lacked signposts. The odd knobbly little green artificial hill, though, hinted at me getting warmer towards my goal in a landscape that got shafted.

Needing to concentrate I turned off the ambience of Faure's 'Cantique de Jean Racine' sung nicely by the local Downside Abbey monks who incidentally were men of minority belief. Not of faith, but of some gratitude being shown toward Baron George Jeffries of Wem, a man that died of kidney disease in his early forties in the Tower of London. Better known as Judge Jeffries the purge of Somerset rebellion, he had also presided at the trial of Titus Oates, a nasty piece of work whose 'porkies' had given rise to one of Downside's martyrs.

Blessed Thomas Pickering was sent to London in 1665 to be steward for the Benedictine monks then chaplains to the Catholic wife of King Charles II. In 1678 Titus fabricated the 'Popish Plot', bearing false witness that Thomas had attempted to shoot the King. The story was believed and Thomas was arrested. Although reprieved by Charles many times, pressure to execute Blessed Thomas was too great, and on 9 May 1679 he was taken to Tyburn where he was hanged, drawn and quartered. In truth all Downside's martyrs seem all to have met a similar fate.

As for Titus, well, he was pilloried, pelted with eggs, stripped and pilloried again, then tied to a cart, and whipped repeatedly over a couple of days before being told off by our infamous judge who called him a "shame to mankind." The process of law has never ceased to amaze me.

Anyway, that's all by the bye. Given the monks sheltered lives I didn't think they'd approve of where I was heading.

Ruth's Arse was on the record, and I couldn't help but try and find it. Had anyone heard of it? No. What about Fry's Bottom? Both were the pits. As we chatted on the road beside a pair of flattened toads, the nice young lady stroked the metal piercing above her chin, and after a pregnant pause that might have put her at risk from pica, she told me to look at a map of Clutton. At her heel, a woolly black mongrel eating something non-nutritious already seemed to have the condition.

Clutton rang a couple of bells. The village had had a character that performed clog dances at local events. He was nicknamed 'Flopper' because instead of swearing, everything was "floppin' this" or "floppin' that." The village was also home to the Rees-Mogg family, a thoughtful lot. They were mine owners against whom strikes were rare, even when the going was tough.

I was in coal country and the lady, I learnt, was a member of a local toad patrol. Every spring she volunteers to help amphibians on their journey to the spawning ponds that were once mine reservoirs, made by damming streams.

"There's Fry's Leaze off Charlcombe Lane," she said trying to be helpful. Fry sleaze?

I decided not to go there. Apparently, Charlcombe Lane was a death trap. Sponsored by Wessex Water, her job was to put toads in buckets and walk them across the road. Some drivers took no notice of diversions and caused toad slaughter. Nodding its head, the mongrel agreed, staring mournfully at the twin corpses of Bufo bufo.

"We're a bit cut off here nowadays. Forgotten almost," she said. I wasn't quick to disagree. The graffiti is the pathos of lost patience. Inside a bus shelter was a red painted human outline, on the outer wall, words daubed from the same pot read, 'Missed You.'

It occurred to me that Mark Twain could have drawn inspiration from a local bloke. "It is easy to find fault if one has that disposition," Twain wrote, "There was once a man who, not being able to find any other fault with his coal, complained that there were too many prehistoric toads in it." Surely he was describing William Smith, The seamer who never bowled a cricket ball. Known both as the 'Father of English Geology' and 'Strata Smith', William sampled and mapped rock layers and collected an array of fossils he found in the Somerset coalfield where coal was rubbish and the seams thin along the Cam Brook, Wellow Brook and Nettlebridge Valleys and around Radstock and Farrington Gurney.

The Romans had warmed to Somerset coal and the third-century writer Solinus makes a somewhat cryptic reference to the temple at Bath, suggesting that coal was burned there. Commercially coal was mined from the fifteenth century. Kilmersdon, however, had been mined since the thirteenth. In autumn 1973 it was also the last pit to close. At the time of nationalisation and the creation of the National Coal Board it was suggested that six Somerset collieries could be worked for at least a hundred years and that new pits could be opened and others re-opened. In the event, only one new pit, Harry Stoke, was opened, and then closed within ten years.

However, evidence of the industry still exists. An old coal mining wheel in front of Radstock museum is the centrepiece of the town described in the *Church Rambler* of 1876-7 as having "all the ugly unwieldiness arising from rapid growth. The frowning chimneys which belch forth smoky blackening and poisoning the fresh pure air of heaven, and the black heaps which load it with grimy dust, mark the mouths of the pits."

When that issue of the *Rambler* went to press, lines of railway and tramways bore coal trucks painted with the name 'Frances Countess of Waldegrave'. The lady herself was a close friend of Edward Lear and a mine-owner trailblazing a new fashion of the peerage becoming connected to 'trade'. "Good heavens," folk must have said, "women will be getting the vote next." Some of those tramways of wonderment are still visible.

At Fry's Bottom in Clutton a stone-lined steep sided tank that was the mine reservoir can be found. Either side of the entrance to Braysdown colliery are grey stone 'olde worlde' looking crenellated follies and a terrace of miners' cottages that screened the unsightly pithead buildings from the eyes of local gentry. On one side the cottages themselves have been gentrified with modern windows and conservatories, while on the other side the cottage windows are breeze-blocked up and the roofs are of rusty corrugated iron.

Braysdown's slag heap is now thickly overgrown with conifers, whereas Paulton's pile, known as "The Batch", looks like a volcano. The village was the terminus of the northern branch of the Somerset Coal Canal and although local entrepreneurs invested heavily in it during the 1790s, it's become a ditch full of brambles and bunnies. Along the line of the canal is Combe Hay, or Cumb as it was called in the *Domesday Book*, where there was a series of locks and, until 1979, a Fuller's Earth mine whose fine-grained clay was used to simulate explosions for film special effects. It made a much bigger plume than ordinary dirt suggesting a larger explosion and allowing a smaller, safer charge to be used.

The coal miners themselves are a dying breed. However, Alex Hann, a retired third generation Somerset miner was recently interviewed by the BBC out of nostalgia. He did fifty years of hot, dusty and dangerous work shared between Kilmersdon and Radstock. Seams less than two-feet wide meant Alex scrabbled on hands and knees in "knickers, a strong pair boots and a hard hat" hacking out the coal a thousand feet down. He was a local legend. Yet he did the job against his dad's wishes, because Tom, Alex's granddad, was killed when a boulder "the size of a double bed" fell on him in 1908. Sadly, deaths in the mines were not uncommon and Alex was philosophical that modern day miners have become technicians instead of men of iron. Hydraulics, electric power, and compressed air now do the 'donkey' work. It was a tough life to be a beast of burden.

In reality horses and ponies became redundant before WWII. By 1938 seven knackered nags were being shared between nine pits. But of all the steeds in the Somerset coalfield Tom, the last 'automatic carthorse', was the most remembered.

Tom worked Norton St Philip's Bell Hill. The steep slope defeated Radstock's coal wagons, so help was needed. At the bottom of the hill, where a garage is today, was the 'Prince Blucher Inn'. So a rope ran from the inn all the way up the hill to ring a stable bell in the courtyard of 'The George' which with an ancestry going back to 1397, if not further, has the undisputed claim to be England's oldest licensed house.

Built of timber frame and soft brick by monks from close by Hinton Priory as a guesthouse, the building goes back to the reign of Plantagenet King Henry III and the first coal was taken out of Kilmersdon. When the Hinton prior allowed the pub's first licence it began a continuity that eventually landed the pub in the *Guinness Book of Records*. The George's venerable age and character made it a useful location for bringing Daniel Defoe's *Moll Flanders* to the silver screen, seeing Morgan Freeman, Robin Wright and Geraldine James plying their acting skills in 1996. And let's not forget Kazou Ishiguro's *Remains of the Day* in 1993 when Anthony Hopkins, Christopher Reeve and Emma Thompson used the pub's atmosphere to boot.

More importantly perhaps, the pub also proved the point that not all men going underground hereabouts were miners. Not long ago, a dowser traced a tunnel from 'The George' to where the Priory stood. Five-feet high and constructed to last, the tunnel hinted at monks sneaking large quantities of booze into the cloisters. A habit that required constitutional reform. From the mid 1500s an alehouse licence could only granted by the Government.

So it was appropriate that in a place of horsehair shirts, the pub's stable was Tom's home. When he heard the bell it was his job to go down the hill on his tod and help a wagon up to the top. Once there Tom would be unhitched and threepence placed in a leather pouch at his head. This was a meagre amount, but in the days before miners' unions what could a carthorse do? With payment made Tom would plod back to his stable under his own volition. No one knows how far back into history this understanding goes, but it was working within living memory. Bell Hill got its name for a reason.

It's an odd thing that all four of my children went through their Somerset school days without ever being told the county had coalmines. History seemed to stop with the Battle of Sedgemoor, long before automatic carthorses. Indeed, that would have been a different story had a Royalist sniper not failed in popping off his target on the morning of the battle. James Scott, Duke of Monmouth, thirty-six years old and the son of Lucy Walter, Charles II's lover, had been watching an early skirmish from a window of 'The George' as he dressed for breakfast. Despite the bullet missing, his day, as my children know, went from bad to worse.

It was not until early afternoon that I found Fry's Bottom, having been delayed at the 'Hunter's Rest', the Clutton pub that was originally built as the Earl of Warwick's hunting lodge in the last years of the eighteenth century. Apparently he had owned a lot of Somerset mines. 'Fry Sleaze', a knowledgable bar bibbler told me, had a rubbish collection on a Thursday. And Ruth's Arse? "Never bloody heard of it. Wish I had, mind," he chuckled.

Unfortunately Fry's Bottom hadn't much to show for itself except for a desultory stone-lined steep-sided tank that was the mine reservoir. A bit boring. But surely there was enough in a name to enthuse pupils to a piece of Somerset heritage that seems to have gone by the board. Something to fill that void of interest between the Bussex Rhyne and The Kooks.

Heading home I listened again to the monks of Downside. It was such a sound of purity.

## DOMINY
# MONSTERS & LIGHT BULBS

*"I have never seen a greater monster or miracle in the world than myself."*

Michel de Montaigne (French Philosopher and Writer, 1533-1592)

"In the west of Somersetshire is a range called the Quantock Hills; it is a wild and picturesque locality, where red deer and black game find a safe retreat; where purple heath and golden furze make the autumnal scene glorious with regal colouring. It is a district where you may walk for miles without passing even a cottage, and where the whortleberry is the only crop. At the eastern side of the Quantock Chain is the parish of Broomfield. Close by the church stands the Manor House, the family seat of the Crosses, called Fyne Court, so named from the manorial fines having been collected there in olden days." These words were written by Cornelia Crosse in 1867. Her father-in-law, a former High Sheriff of Somerset, rather blotted his copybook by mounting the tricolour, and standing upon the ruins of the Bastille the day it was captured. Hell, he was a republican.

Cornelia's hubby Andrew, like his dad, didn't keep his politics to himself. A 'sparky' and a prophet, he came out with the little gem, "by means of the electric agency, we shall be enabled to communicate our thoughts instantaneously with the uttermost ends of the earth." Dangerous talk that at the time seemed a load of twaddle. This was not helped by the story of the parish 'money field'. Wealth, it's said, was within a castle of iron, guarded by spirits. True, once upon a time an underground passage did exist, but it was closed up in the dim and distant past, and the field planted over with spuds, elephant grass or rape. Legend, though, has it that a door to the castle could be found at a full moon. Sadly, a hopeful friend, even with the hallucinogen of a scrumpy gut-load, found nowt but starlight.

Trying to put a perspective on things, I first came upon the name of Broomfield while making a short documentary called 'Pebble and Feather'. Rumour had it that Andrew had inspired Mary Shelley to write 'Frankenstein'. For me this was an important connection. Broomfield was a seriously important place. My film was about how spirituality can help overcome extreme trauma.

The camera followed me walking straw-hatted in Egypt among Aswan's crimson bougainvillea flowers. Behind me feluccas flapped lateen sails on the River Nile whose source at Ripon Falls, on Uganda's Lake Victoria, had been traced in 1862 by John Hanning Speke, a controversial Somerset gentleman from Dowlish Wake. "The Nile is settled," said his telegram sent from Khartoum to the Royal Geographical Society of London.

Somerset conditioned too, my ears absorbed a familiar burr sounding like "Ooooh-arrrrrr, whatta-whatta-lump-a-Chard." Couldn't be. With a lug rub, all was well. I was just hearing loud-speakers on minarets blaring the call to prayer. Then, as egrets flapped in the Nile-side trees, I narrated words written in what now feels like a past age: "She called me her Lazarus. Born again. Heart transplanted. To me, I was Shelley's monster, cut, compassion craving. A mind of feeling, but Frankenstein torn. Saved from decay. Dust delayed, Different."

This was earnest stuff that was to be premiered at the annual docu-mentary film festival in Moldova's capital, Chisinau. Fate had turned my life on its head. So, I thought an actual visit to Broomfield probably wouldn't do any harm. But I had mixed feelings.

Alfred Bowerman was born in the village in 1873. Although a Bridgwater timber merchant by trade, he became better known in his day as a cricketer. Admittedly, his time at Somerset County Cricket Club wasn't very auspicious, scoring just 8 runs in 4 innings and taking one catch in the two games he played. However, Alfred does have a claim to fame. He took the field for the Devon Wanderers team that represented Great Britain in the 1900 Summer Olympics cricket competition, the only time that cricket has featured in the Olympics. In the only game against France, Alfred scored 7 in the first innings, and 59 in the second, the top score of the match, as Great Britain picked up the gold medal.

More poignantly for me, The Clash vocalist Joe Strummer died as the victim of an undiagnosed congenital heart defect at his home there in December 2002 aged 50. This was ironic, as Broomfield was famed in the *Domesday Book* for the longevity of its inhabitants. In punk music parlance it's said that whereas The Sex Pistols made people hit their heads against a wall, The Clash made them do it for a reason. I was more restrained and just pogoed up and down.

Joe had adopted Bridgwater as his hometown. His reason for that was down to Somerset-based filmmaker, Julien Temple, who took my seat on the board of the charity Somerset Film and Video when poorly times had resigned me to Egypt.

Julien had mixed with both The Sex Pistols and The Clash, before he directed the film *Pandaemonium*. Filmed on the Quantocks and Nettlecombe, it was about a villainous William Wordsworth trying to sabotage one-time best friend Samuel Taylor Coleridge's career, tricking him into burning the manuscript of 'Kubla Khan.' Fortunately, an opium-fried, insane Dorothy Wordsworth, William's sister, had committed the poetic fragment to memory. The film ends with Samuel reading the published poem to his kids. A fractured literary history that now sits on my shelf of DVDs.

However, Julien also directed *The Future Is Unwritten*, a documentary about Joe's life, and was responsible for introducing Joe to Bridgwater when he first moved to the county.

"It was the Carnival," Julien recalled, "and the first thing that happened was a float came round the corner with 'Rock the Casbah' and all these people in Arabian Nights costumes. About twenty minutes later a 'Should I Stay or Should I Go' float came round the corner and he was like 'I love this, this is a Clash town, I love this town, I want to live here' which he did. And he did love the town, and I think he understood that it was in need of some affectionate care and help, because other places in the South West received a lot more attention than Bridgwater."

Joe played his last gig to a sell-out crowd at 'the Palace', the town's smallish nightclub, a month before his death. The golden moment was when Joe got a tad fired up. Taking off his famous battered old guitar, he threw it hard to the side of the stage at one of the roadies who did well to catch and hold on to it. Joe acknowledged his gratitude by turning and giving the chap the thumbs up. Sadly, there was no 'White Riot', which was the name of my University 5-a-side football team and The Clash tune we had played before each of our matches. Needless to say, in a PC age we got heckled a lot. Something we countered by enlisting the services of Gladstone, a Nigerian law and politics student who ripped the caps off beer bottles with his teeth.

Joe's friends, that include Damien Hirst, say he was passionate about trying to revitalise Bridgwater and in his remembrance, have established the Strummerville Foundation for the promotion of new music and help for young musicians. And he's not just remembered in the music world. On 12 February 2005 the Class 47 locomotive 47828 was named "Joe Strummer" at a ceremony at Bristol Temple Meads railway station.

I took myself off to Broomfield in February as new lambs began their freedom bounce. In the road outside the church a pony-tailed lady in a bright blue anorak was shouting confusion. "No Danni! Good girl!" Not that a large shaggy mutt was paying any attention to her, preferring instead frolic with an arm-flapping postman collecting mail from the letterbox by the churchyard wall. Eventually the envelopes were bagged-up bearing muddy paw marks. Unseen, a stone gate-pillar carving of a small Green Man like character grinned toothily.

A small glove on an old gate hinge and another, bigger, on the spiked railing of Fyne Court Farm's front garden exhibited the losses of the cold snap that had relented. Through the flimsy wrought iron gate, latched by a large bent rusty nail, snowdrops had opened into parasols tempting the first bright suns of celandines to appear beside the church path.

The yew tree, that a local told me was the biggest in the county, looked in fine fettle.

The church itself was a Gothic sight. Winged and clawed demons dribbled from their mouths while other hunkypunks appeared to scream. Hanging from an aerial below the church tower's weathervane were a symbolic myriad of non-energy efficient light bulbs attached to a rats-nest tangle of wires. It was the first sign of recognition I'd seen for the man buried in the shade of a large holly bush in a churchyard corner.

His grave was marked by an stumpy obelisk inscribed "Sacred to the memory of Andrew Crosse, Electrician. He was humble towards God and kind to his fellow creatures." I recited the poetic words of Janet Paterson Frame in my head. "Electricity, the peril the wind sings to in the wires on a grey day." Andrew might have appreciated them.

So what about the chap? Well, he was active in party politics advocating the benefits of education for the lower classes, arguing against emigration, and supporting the campaign by local farmers against falling food prices and high taxes during the 1820s. Following the Battle of Waterloo, Andrew boarded a ship at Exeter and was able to see the captured Napoleon Bonaparte on the deck of HMS *Bellerophon*, a ship whose timber would be recycled as the Downside Priory organ.

He also fancied himself as a lawyer. However, like me he gave up on that idea. Only he went on to do something useful, recreating himself as a scientist with a penchant for poetry. This was the chemistry that, if the gossip is to be believed, led to laden bookshelves and Hollywood box-office attractions for those who enjoy the horror genre.

On a small wooden table Andrew accidentally 'created life-forms' when all he was attempting to do was to make crystals. The 1911 edition of the *Encyclopedia Britannica* makes it known that along with Sir Humphrey Davy, who visited Fyne Court in 1827, Andrew was one of the first to develop large voltaic piles. They could charge and discharge twenty times a minute, "accompanied by reports almost as loud as those of a cannon." Such spectacular dabblings got him the local nickname of 'the thunder and lightning man'. Local farmers blamed him for the blight of the wheat crop and commissioned an exorcism in the nearby hills.

Then in the 1830s the legend began. Andrew had been conducting an electro-crystallization experiment when, on its twenty-sixth day he saw what he described as "the perfect insect, standing erect on a few bristles which formed its tail."

All he had used to achieve this was a shelved wooden frame, a funnel of Wedgwood ware, inside which a fluid filled quart basin rested on a circular piece of mahogany, a wetted strip of flannel, and perhaps most importantly, a piece of red iron oxide from Mount Vesuvius. This stone was kept constantly electrified by a Voltaic battery of zinc and copper plates sitting in two porcelain troughs. At first Crosse filled the cells with both and water and a minute amount of hydrochloric acid, but at the time of his wonderment merely with drinking water. Not quite your modern Duracell.

More creatures appeared and two days later they moved their legs. Andrew was stumped. A thorough search of dusty nooks, crannies and corners revealed a complete lack of bugdom. Yet over the next few weeks, hundreds more magically materialised and all were averse to sunlight. They crawled around the table and hid themselves when they could find a shelter. Puzzled by the results, Andrew mentioned the incident to a couple of friends. He also sent the results to the London Electrical Society reporting, "I examined them with the microscope, and observed that the smaller ones appeared to have only 6 legs, but the larger ones 8…It seems that they are of a species not hitherto observed…I beg that it might be understood that I do not mean creation, or any thing approaching it."

A local newspaper learned of the incident and published an article about the "extraordinary experiment" and named the insects *Acarus crossii*. The article was subsequently picked up elsewhere across the country and in Europe. Some of the readers apparently gained the impression that Andrew had somehow "created" the insects or at least claimed to have done so. He received angry letters in which he was accused of blasphemy and trying to take God's place as a creator. Some of them included death threats. Despite attempts elsewhere no other scientists could replicate Andrew's results.

So it was hardly surprising, folk speculated, that Andrew inspired *Frankenstein*.

Mary Shelley and Andrew did know each other through a mutual friend, the poet Robert Southey. Also, Bysshe Shelley and Mary attended a lecture by Andrew in December 1814 in London, during which he explained his experiments with atmospheric electricity. As a clincher, the local journo Edward W. Cox wrote a report in the *Taunton Courier* in Autumn 1836 about Mary's visits to Broomfield to see Andrew's work.

Recently Somerset County Council bought a couple of Andrew's letters at auction for £400. Both talk about "some products formed in a new manner" and also speak of a desire to see the work being conducted into "animal magnetism". They can be viewed free of charge in the Record Office.

Nobody at the time seemed willing to accept Andrew's mundane explanation that his 'creations' were just insect eggs embedded in his samples. It was only later that killjoys agreed that the insects were probably cheese mites from Andrew's snacks on the job that had contaminated his instruments. Proof, if proof was needed, that Somerset cheddar can be the stuff of nightmares.

The infamous laboratory table now sits in the nave of Broomfield church. Upon it, I found the visitors book encrusted with candle wax. All very atmospheric. Out of nosiness, I turned a few pages and found an interesting entry.

"11/10/08 Tim Hills Local Yew Group www.ancient-yew.org. Sorry to disappoint, but there are many yews in Somerset larger than your fine specimen. Go to our website. It is good to see your tree in such good health."

In a place where I had laid a personal ghost to rest, it was about time Broomfield had a new cause of monster debate.

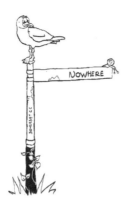

## DIK
# UNSUNG & SILENT

*"Brave men are all vertebrates; they have their softness on the surface and their toughness in the middle."*

Gilbert Keith Chesterton (Novelist and Poet, 1874-1936)

In the first week of June getting home from visiting family in Cologne meant a flight change in Holland, and I found the Dutch milking it. At Amsterdam's Schiphol airport every passing Englishman was asked if they liked cricket by a gloating gent selling *The Times*. This was a bad omen. A glutton for punishment, I spent my last euro.

You could have struck me down with a feather duster.

Turn one's back for a day and without a bye or leave balances tilt. The 'Orangemen' had beaten England's finest at Twenty20 in pouring rain under the floodlights of Lords. Yes, I read that twice. Well, I suppose we had it coming. As far back as the mid sixteenth-century Glastonbury had been settled by Flemish weavers who were described as "kings of crekettes." who used "wickettes." It is thought the weavers brought cricket to England and played it close to where they looked after their sheep, using shepherd's crooks as bats. Indeed, in 1533 the poet John Skelton put early woes into words:

"THE IMAGE OF IPOCRISIE
O lodre of Ipocrites,
Nowe shut vpp your wickettes,
And clappe to your clickettes!
A! Farewell, kings of crekettes!

And in need of council, Somerset had got the blues, political oranges were bitter, and labour had never left the pub. What Status Quo remained readied to play Glastonbury.

Calm, I thought. Oblivious to it all, hobbies on the wing would still be catching hatching dragonfly nymphs on Shapwick Heath and a certain strip of tarmac would remain unfinished. Providing a border between open pasture and Burnham estates of new-builds, with arty-fart road names like Ben Travers Way, Stoppard Road, Shaw Walk, and Wilde Close, lay a bone of contention.

A spur off Love Lane, and nicknamed "the road to nowhere," the Frank Foley Parkway ends abruptly in a field. Local MP, David Heathcoat-Amory, blamed this bafflement on the "lunatics" of Somerset County Council's road planning department. To try and get things sorted out, he had joined forces with Burnham and Highbridge Town Council. Matters shouldn't be left to fester.

So, unsurprisingly, when an early day motion raised by Russell Brown, a Scottish MP, sought to rectify a misjustice done to a chap born in Highbridge called Frank Foley, the name rang a bell. Something was amiss, especially when diplomacy landed Cherie Blair, the wife of the United Nations' Middle East envoy in a gathering with a London Rabbi and a committee of Highbridge townsfolk to scrutinise a plaque unveiled in a flowerbed full of pansies. Catholic Cherie was in earnest mood speaking on how religious divisions should be put aside, and why people should live together as one united community.

Among Cherie's small crowd was movie producer Timothy Haas, of the independent production company Haas-Silver-Levene. Although still in the process making a film on Lord Haw-Haw, Timothy has recently begun work on creating 'a new blockbuster' about the life of Frank Foley.

Sadly, although reported on 'TotallyJewish.com' the story got lost locally when newsrooms were distracted by a letter in the window of Highbridge Children's Centre addressed to the "horrible people" that broke the glass and stole a computer. Asking the burglars to come and say sorry, the letter read: "We are very upset, angry, sad and cross that our window has been broken. We couldn't play in our nursery today because you broke our window." All the children had signed it.

Certainly, the tears of innocents were a distraction from asking who the guy was that attracted the attention of government. It would be correct to have described him as an overweight and middle-aged British bureaucrat, with round, owlish glasses hovering below a balding head and who loved gardening. But in truth, Frank was so much more than that. I mean, for goodness sake, there was a gurt great lump of a statue to him.

It stands on the 'town green', a small area of bare-patched and daisied grass opposite the 'One-Stop-Shop', about the only place in Market Street that's not tatty and shuttered-up. However, the lady on the till said she worked ten hours a day and barely had time to look at the artwork, let alone know anything about the thing.

Most odd, I thought. Passing it every time I go to the fishing tackle shop, the statue had been there since mid 2005. Eight-feet high and sculpted out of Portland stone by stone carver Jonathan Sells, a man of strangely shaven beard, the statue was conspicuous by its whiteness. It had taken £25,000 raised over five years through dinner dances, street parties, bring-and-buy sales and fetes to be able to commission the piece that was supposed to have put Highbridge on the map. Local buildings were depicted, such as the town's clock and bridge, and, most importantly, someone in spectacles signing a document for a man and child.

That 'someone' was Major Francis Edward Foley who MI6 recognise as one of its greatest officers. This quiet and modest man was Britain's top spy in Berlin and in his 'cover' job as Passport Control Officer in Berlin, according to one Jewish aid worker, saved "tens of thousands" of people from the Holocaust by having the guts to bend the rules. Which to be fair, is something Somerset folk have always been very good at. His work was even more remarkable given that he was running a major intelligence operation, acquiring details of most of Germany's military research and development that were eventually crucial to Allied victory.

Frank was described by Margaret Reid, a member of the M16 support staff, in a letter to her mum, as "an active little man, wears a Harris Tweed jacket and appears to work 14 hours a day and remains good-tempered. He is not at all terrifying to work for." This was a fellow who through his known and active hostility to the Nazi regime created an ingenious double bluff that concealed his spying operations and let him do what he was morally drawn to. The whole Hitler regime was anathema to Frank. He said, "it was the rule of the devil on earth".

Truth was that thousands of Jewish families with documents and visas faked by Frank escaped from Nazi Germany after Kristallnacht, the Night of Broken Glass, the anti-Jewish pogrom on 9th and 10th November 1938, and before the outbreak of the Second World War. Not until after the War's end did they become aware of the identity of their life saving benefactor.

Benno Cohen, the former Chairman of the German Zionist Organisation when speaking out about the reign of terror and how few people had reached out to help the Jews, said, "There was one man who stood out above all others like a beacon. Captain Foley, Passport Officer in the British Consulate in the Tiergarten in Berlin, a man who in my opinion was one of the greatest among the nations of the world. He brought his influence to bear to help us. It was possible to bring a great number of people to Israel through the help of his most wonderful person. He rescued thousands of Jews from the jaws of death."

When Frank passed on in 1958, the Jewish people planted a memorial grove in his honour in the hills of Jerusalem. Each of the thousands of trees in that grove was paid for by someone he had saved. His name is also inscribed on the Holocaust memorial at Yad Vashem in Israel.

In 1999, Frank was awarded the title of Righteous Among the Nations, the highest honour the Jewish people can grant a gentile. In a letter to the *Jerusalem Post* welcoming the decision, one of those he helped wrote: "I myself have five children and 18 grandchildren, none of whom would have ever seen the light of day had I not lived. There are countless men, women and children today who would never have been born but for Foley. May god bless his memory."

High time then for Frank to be recognised by his hometown. Of course he was, but unfortunately the Highbridge statue was put in place a year too late. Up in the Black Country, having perhaps got wind of frantic westerly chiselings, Stourbridge had already had the cheek to claim Frank as theirs, calling him 'the Stourbridge Schindler'. A plaque at the entrance to their Mary Stevens Park names him as 'a Stourbridge man'. As mysterious as Frank's life, this was as much rubbish as Worcestershire and Durham hailing Sir Ian Botham as their own.

They got their plaque on show shortly after Jack Straw, then Foreign Secretary, praised Frank Foley's heroism during a commemorative event in Berlin. He announced: "Frank Foley risked his life to save the lives of thousands of German Jews. Without the protection of diplomatic immunity he visited internment camps and sheltered Jewish refugees in his house. Frank Foley was a true British hero." It was the first time that the British government had officially recognised Frank's bravery. No mention though was given to Frank's beloved wife, Kay, who was steadfast and helpful beside him throughout. That job was to rest with the *Daily Telegraph's* Defence Correspondent Michael Smith, whose book *Foley – The spy who saved 10,000 Jews*, first brought Frank's deeds to light. Michael had come across Frank by accident while writing a history of British espionage.

"One of the most interesting things about Foley," a former agent told Michael, "was that normally, to be a good case officer, you have to be a bit of a shit. But Foley managed to be a good case officer and a near saint. He was a quite outstanding character. Schindler pales into insignificance alongside his work. He was a very, very able man who I don't think ever got the recognition he deserved."

So to put things straight, Frank, the third of five children, was born in 1884 at 7 Walrow Terrace, a two-up, two-down railway worker's house, in little Highbridge. A plaque on the house wall says so. His dad, Andrew Wood Foley, no relation to your author, was one of 250 workers at the 'extensive locomotive works' that the Somerset and Dorset Joint Railway Company had just built to maintain their blue-engined locomotives. Frank's mum Isabella, a devout Catholic, had him educated by the French La Retraite order of nuns at Burnham's St. Joseph's Roman Catholic School. When the nuns' influence prompted Frank to say he wanted to become a priest, his dad told him that it would be a waste of time. Much better, he advised, to make something of one's life. Frank took those words of wisdom to heart.

However fascinating his Berlin life might have been, remarkably it was just one episode in several high profile roles that he played during War. Following his departure from Germany at the War's outbreak he was moved to Norway. Once there he soon became a key figure in the plot to save the Norwegian King Haakon VII and defend the country from German invasion.

Although King Haakon eventually moved to Britain and the country was over-run, Frank did his utmost to persuade the British government to intervene and was awarded one of Norway's highest medals in recognition of his efforts.

Back in Blighty himself, Frank continued to run wartime agents in Norway. He became one of the few to debrief Hitler's Deputy, Rudolf Hess, after his flight to Britain bearing gifts of monkey-puzzle trees. Subsequently, Frank became intimately involved in Operation Doublecross, the scheme to turn agents around the world to work for Britain against the Nazis.

As part of this massive ruse of disinformation, he was complicit in Operation 'Mincemeat' the now famous plot of getting hold of a human cadaver, dressing it as a 'Major William Martin, R.M.' and putting it into the sea near Huelva, Spain. Attached to the corpse was a brief-case containing fake letters suggesting that Allied attacks would land in Sardinia and Greece. The ploy was so successful that the Germans still believed that Sardinia and Greece were the intended objectives, weeks after 'Operation 'Husky', the Allied invasion of Sicily had begun. Unsurprisingly, Frank Foley wasn't mentioned in *The Man Who Never Was* the film of the story, directed by Ronald Neame, which entered into the 1956 Cannes Film Festival.

And this wasn't all. Frank also had a crucial role in frustrating various schemes of the Stalinist Comintern, acquiring double agents who, for example, prevented a pro-Russian coup in Brazil.

So be proud, Highbridge. Be very, very proud. Show it and maybe the newly elected Somerset County Council will feel obliged to finish the road that Frank might with a wry smile have modestly called an 'autobahn'.

And the plaque amid the pansies? Well, it's at the Sternberg Centre in Finchley, North London and reads:

To the righteous memory of
Frank Foley
Born 28.11.1884 – Died 08.05.1958
He served in the
British Passport Office, Berlin
1920 – 1939

Jewish Tradition declares:

"He who saves a single life, it is as if he had saved the whole world."

Frank Foley saved the lives of 11,000 Jews between 1933 and 1939.

11,000? Perhaps among Cherie's crowd there was a fisherman who liked to exaggerate. But then again, there's a commonly held belief that anglers, like gardeners, are warm-hearted people. Whilst Pam Lyes, the secretary of Highbridge's Frank Foley committee said, "Cherie was wonderful," ordinary member John Curtis, wanted it remembered that Frank was the best of British and "should be much more celebrated in this country and his story used for education in our schools."

Hopefully, Timothy Haas's film, if completed, will be accurate. It has every chance to be, as his mum, Eve, was brought out of Germany with Frank's help.

## HAINDIK
# TWIN HULLS & HOOF GLUE

*"If all politicians fished instead of spoke publicly, we would be at peace with the world."*

Will Rogers (American entertainer, 1879-1935)

Three African pygmy hedgehogs, all twitchy-nosed and quarter the size of Somerset fuz-pigs, had been rescued by a Wellington fireman. "They were smoky and a bit wet but otherwise alright. They were very quiet for a while but then one of them hissed at me, so I realised they must be okay." His comments came as he was surrounded by a whiff of charred fish. The pygmies were the pets of Sam Cunningham, manager of 'Don Jones Fresh Fish' that had been voted best fishmongers in the country. Sam's shop was no more. Pyromaniac youths had lit a fire in an adjoining row of derelict houses that had spread.

Looking at the travesty, Sam wore a haunted look. He was out of business. "It was quite a sight. Slate was exploding and bits of cob wall were flying off," he told reporters.

What to do? Weighing up the option of Tesco's, I decided to catch my own. Though not for me, expensive trouting in the Barle with licensed bites of mosquito and midge. Mass attacks from those airborne piranhas reminded me I was not as high up on the food chain as I thought. It was best to seek insect free open seas and receive nibbles instead from codling and beasts of greater substance. And by taking out the middlemen, what's in the sea is free. Although a novice, I had salt-watered before, uptide dangling out of Porlock Weir with Deaf Derek, but this was never serious stuff, and also from Minehead, in the top three cod ports in the country for anglers.

This knowledge was imparted by the fish man under a tarpaulin stand at Minehead's Friday farmer's market, where he sold self-caught cod, brill, whiting and mullet. He inspired me to prepare myself in good time with lugworms loosely wrapped in newspaper taking up fridge space above the Milano salami and prosciutto cotto. After the fish man's tip and chuckle, the experience was then magic. That it is to say, the name of the boat was *Magic*.

Potentially the skipper, John Lush, might have added expertise to a perpetual series of occasions for hope. But no. A former secondary school teacher, who by mutual agreement had abandoned the classroom, Lush was as thin as an eight foot boat rod, and with his love for dragging an illicit substance, many times as high. His delight was to dance naked on the cabin roof, causing horizon gazing Butlinites to either believe they were witnessing a quaint Somerset custom, or to go back to their rooms to check bottle labels. Those aboard had the whiff of reason for Lush's fresh air desire. Feeling the cramp of the cabin Lush had the urge for a movement, but missed the bucket on the floor. His favourite saying was 'caution is a most valuable asset in fishing, especially if you are the fish'. First impressions can be like that. Lush's eight-year-old son, forever fumbled as the embarrassed boat-hand.

Needless to say, aboard *Magic*, I never caught a codling. Too much distraction, not helped by Lush's story of some islands called the Green Meadows of Enchantment. He noticed my furrowed brow and followed my stare out toward Flat Holm and Steep Holm, and told me not to be 'stupid'. Apparently, he meant the fairy islands not usually visible to humans, and certainly not to those that sought them, that lay somewhere between Somerset and Pembrokeshire. Of the two, the fairies chose to do their shopping in Wales.

Lush was adamant the Green Meadows could be seen from the air. Given how high he actually was, I didn't think this surprising. My scepticism was apparent, so he tried another attempt to convince me. During the last century some sailors claimed to have landed on the Green Meadows and joined in fairy shenanigans. However, after the sailors got back on their boat and looked back, the islands had vanished. One day, Lush vanished, too. A few locals say he was spirited away by the fairies, others that he emigrated.

Left thinking where best to find fish of substance, a more grounded wreck gave me inspiration. At a point forming an imagined triangle with the shadowy behemoth that is nuclear Hinkley B and Steep Holm, I discovered the skeletal SS *Nornen*. Get-at-able at low tide, it lies across sands that are worked by industrious lugworms, stained with Welsh coal dust, and imprinted with horses' hooves. To me this was a timeless place, until some dune hugging 4 x 4's made their statement that nowhere is safe.

The *Nornen*, a Norwegian barque, ran aground on Berrow beach in 1897 and had its crew and dog saved by the ten oarsmen of the Burnham lifeboat *The John Godfrey Morris*. From one of the seaweed smothered wooden ribs a lone gull, now captain and 'last man' aboard, eyed me dismissively, in much the same way as its human predecessor maybe took a trio of lighthouses at Burnham to be hallucination. What small coastal town has three lighthouses? Well, by accident Burnham did – a defunct round masonry tower, a hundred foot high brick pillar that wasn't up to it, and a wooden one on nine stilts, painted white with a red stripe, stuck on the sands.

Of the three, the tower is the oldest, and is a story of 'good works'. In the last decade of the eighteenth century, a fisherman and his wife lived near the church in a cottage looking out to sea. Getting a bad vibe about her husband's safety during a gale-bashed Burnham night, the wife had the inspiration to put a candle in their cottage window, a guiding light home that was the salvation of the fisherman and his fellows. Along with the wife getting a big hug, the grateful matelots decided to pay her the occasional penny from then on to keep a candle burning. This was observed by the church sexton who in turn offered the fisherman's wife five pounds for the rights to place a light on the church tower, it being closer to God and all that. Then the sexton was given twenty quid by the Reverend David Davies, Burnham's curate, who had the castellated edifice built known today as the Round Tower. All proving that back then even the humble candle could elicit matters of class.

The tower found itself reduced by half so as not to be confused by boat captains when a new erection became the paraffin-lamped 'Pillar of Burnham' in the 1830s, on what is now the busy Berrow Road. However, although through stubbornness the light was not turned off until 1993, the architect had suffered an aberration. Some wise-guy pointed out the 'loightarse' wasn't high enough to do its job properly given the massive rise and fall of the tides. The result? Great popu-larity with grockles wanting to gawp at Wales and Deb'n, and, in 1832, the need for another lighthouse. A 'complimentary one', embarrassed folk called it. Just over thirty feet high and still active, the beach lighthouse continues to fascinate beach-walkers and fills many a camera lens.

Just around the corner from it, beside the Nornen, my attention was grabbed by a five-yard wide dense strip of small, brightly coloured seashells, in hues of yellow, orange and blue, like spilled treasure just in front of the wreck. Nowhere else on the beach are they in such numbers. I remembered, that fish also had a liking for wrecks. Not so much one beached due to careless driving but those in deeper water. So I joined in monthly raids on the shipping lanes with a band of good Somerset men.

We were an eclectic bunch. 'Honest John', the singing surgeon; absent-minded Ray of the untidy tackle box of useless junk, botanist, and seed merchant; Anthony, the Somerset adopted Aussie pharmacist, escaping his allotment rotavator; Dave-the-Graphic, escaping Bristol, lugging a large ice-box and cuddling his digital SLR camera; two GPs, Mark the Trike and flat-capped Big Jeremy, both escaping the sea of human misery that entered one by one daily through the surgery door; Martin, a one time blacksmith, and Chris, his hardened bass-murdering son who resembles one of the Krays; the indescribable me; and Puking Paul, for whom there was collective concern upon the twin-hulled boat that was *Gemini*.

I had replaced Consultant pathologist, 'Sea-Pee'. He was mortified when Martin accidentally sat on his spectacles eighteen miles offshore. See-Pee's black humour was a loss, the boat having been a sanctuary from his frustrations. Something I had deduced over a dinner party chat.

See-Pee's young son was once asked in a class 'stand and tell' period what his father did for work. 'My Daddy looks at dead people through a telescope,' came the reply. This was pretty close to the truth. On Thursdays at Taunton's Musgrove Park Hospital he dons chain mail gloves, costing tens of thousands of pounds a pair, and has a 'cut up'. In posh hospitals it's called 'trimming'. Other days invariably held nothing but boredom. His job involved overseeing a room four times the size of a large conservatory where ten women spend their time staring down microscopes at cervical smears, with the only sound being the occasional 'menstrual disturbance'.

Indeed, the ways of women were his bugbear, becoming animated about 'the galleons of the night,' honey-monster nurses surviving on sweets and biscuits. One can only imagine his reaction on turning up to *Gemini* only to find a woman of similar build aboard. The one and only woman ever to be throbbed by the boat's motors, she was a whinging drug rep of minimal humour, and a destabilising risk to the convivial relationship between man and sea. Who had invited her is now a closed book. However, the look on her face, when the large hand of Martin goosed her from behind, became likened to the legends of Lush.

For Sea-Pee meanwhile, the unfortunate's fate was nothing compared to what he wished upon the women volunteers in the League of Friends Shop, who, to use his words, 'enjoyed their last job before demising.' He blamed one of these ladies for "the world's most stupid conversation." Being in the queue behind the ward collection of *Suns*, sweet, biscuits and drinks had not helped his patience, when all he wanted was *The New Scientist*. Handing over a £10 note he was given back a handful of loose change. Seeing a £5 in the till, Sea-Pee pointed to it, and asked if he could have it instead of the many coins. "No," said the lady belligerently.

"Why not?"

"It's my last one."

"So?"

"I might need it."

This was at the start of a bad week during which a Coroner's official requested, without any relevant notes, that Sea-Pee identify 'one body, nobody, could have been anybody, found on top of the 'Prince of Wales'.

Twenty-four hours later, it was red faces all round at a Coroner's inquest when 'a death by pneumonia' was actually found with a plastic bin bag over the head. Added to this, a member of family stood up and asked, 'What about the suicide notes?' After that, following the cremation of an 'innocent' canal drowning, the police thought actually it might have been murder. They left it for Sea-Pee to decide. The only tissue remaining consisted of the size of two after dinner mints. Then come 'cut-up day' his trainee couldn't do an important cardio-vascular presentation because of the arrival of a garden shed. Friday, saw his colleague, Carlos, reported for smoking outside the morgue by a member of hospital staff who no doubt felt public spirited. Carlos nominated the snitch for the 'employee of the month' award, while he himself became recognisable as a lone figure lighting up in the adjacent cemetery where one can lose all track of time.

Sea-Pee must miss the early morning ploughing through spray crochet and crystal drops, I thought, gripping my rod, a bankstick apparently. Beside me, Paul chuddered over the rail. This had once been a technique used by my son, Felix, for catching mackerel after a breakfast of strawberries and cream. Within seconds he had caught four on a line, with nothing before or after.

As sun spangled the water, Honest John ceased his loud song from the golden age of flower-power that had seemed a tad incongruous at sea, and suddenly became Hemingway. "It's a Marlin! No it's not, it's Mr Ling. No it's not, it's Mr Pollack, No it's not, it's ...Charles."

Entangled, I got a nudge from Martin, a man who bored of blacksmithing, had turned his forge heat over to bashing out special technical parts for Aston Martin, as well as making Mark's trike used for visiting rural patients. 'New rod? Pre War?' Martin queried.

'Vintage and car-booted. Rod and reel car for not a lot. It's what's on the end that's important.' I said, showing off my rubbery orange and custard sidewinder lure.

Martin's laugh was noticed by Dave Harrington, the skipper.

Dave, a silver-haired Yorkshireman from the school-of-hard-knocks is of temperamental mood. Anyone thumping lead weights against his windows proved it. He had much cabin gadgetry. The technological hunted the biological, and we all secretly admitted it was Dave, not us, that caught the fish. John though was already winding him up in the alternative sport of the day. 'It's whaa-tin', tin it, Dave? It's whaa-tin'.' Which translated as: 'It is whiting, is not, Dave? It is whiting.' Dave had translated it, too, and scowled. His eyes then fell on me.

"Whaddya call tha'?"

"It's a rod, Dave," I replied, "John sold it me for a tenner." Inwardly, I acknowledged my pride seemed out of place amongst the eclectic gathering of elitism and that Honest John delighted in life's little profits.

"Tha' fishin' pole is a stick with a hook at one end and a fool on t'other."

"Samuel Johnson?" I asked.

"Nah, you. You were robbed. Too short, too stiff. Better you take it home and grow beans up it. And the reel? Phoar, rubbish! No good them. No good 'tall."

Mick, his boat hand, a weathered dead-ringer for actor Timothy Spall, in yellow fisherman's trousers and sporting a brass Scottie dog on his scale encrusted cap, agreed with him. Sunny disposition had returned at my expense. Stubborn, I turned my back and let gravity take the weight.

True, the rod was made in pre carbon-fibre and graphite days, and it bore not a single colourful logo. But the eyes looked nice, lashed on with lacquered twine, and the beech steel-tipped handle with a touch of rust was comfortable. And yes, the reel with its yellowed nylon line was, in all fairness, a little old-fashioned compared to today's engineering marvels.

Dave's smile became palpable as the line began to birds-nest on reel spool and began unscrewing itself from the rod-stick as the line suddenly went taut. It was a five-minute tussle from which I emerged victorious with orange and custard consumed by a pollack.

Like me, Honest John was ecstatic and gave the rod a nod. "Charles, Charles, Charles, you musn't believe what those two tell you. They're just a pair of tackle tarts. What are you going to do with it?"

"I'm going to mount it on the landing wall, above my granddad's Cambridge oar, with a brown parcel tag tied to an eye saying, 'Mr. Pollack 1st April 2009.'" Or should it be 'colin'? Sainsbury's supermarkets around Somerset, in an attempt to prise folk away from long suffering cod, were trying to reinvent pollack by making it sound more appetising. Claiming that shoppers were embarrassed to buy something that sounded like bollocks, or a member of the sizable Polish community, colin, a corruption of 'colan', the French for pollack, would do the job. Daft. Hadn't Sainbury's heard what a 'colon' did? Better to call it Gilbert.

Then my rod handle fell off, the day's stress all too much for the ancient hoof glue.

"No worries," said Ray and produced from his untidy tackle box a small tube of super stuff that could bond a wooden rod to a boat-deck in a second.

From Honest John came a smile; from Dave a squawk, a wondrous imitation of a herring gull amid the fishy slaughter from which I had suddenly ceased to be a part.

Ray, bless him, was persevering with ling, a fish obviously a cross between a cod and a conger. "Is it a codonger? Or, a congcod? Or, just a longer cod?" he mused. It was joyful to see his facial contortions, having reeled in a large male that rudely performed the notorious hang-man's ejaculation down his trousers. As the seed merchant dispatched the fish with a hardy priest, John observed that Ray appeared over-excited.

However, extreme fishing is what Ray is about. A piranha skull hangs from his garden cider apple tree. Getting it there had been an adventure. As gulls, gannets and skuas screamed above Ray's 'live' ling bait cocktails of stinky mackerel, squid and Burnham sand eel, he revealed the story. The skull was a trophy from a trip up the Amazon. As soon as he caught the little teeth-gnasher, he wanted a tangible memory to take home.

After severance, Ray placed the head in a plastic bag, before wrapping it within another, and then another, sealing the parcel with heavy-duty adhesive tape. Back in his third floor hotel room some time had passed, and the head rotting began to smell. Ray, thinking it best to sterilise it, placed the package in the courtesy microwave and pushed the 'on' button. The explosion that followed blew off the oven door, and the ensuing stench permeated the corridor prompting the opening of doors and much retching. "It was a bit pongy," Ray admitted, "If you bottled the smell it could have substituted for gas in the trenches." Not wanting to be found culprit and on hearing frantic activity from hotel staff, he lowered the head out of the window on a length of fishing twine, provoking repeated inquest on the level below. Eventually, disguised in a suitcase amid the smell of the rest of his fishing equipment the skull reached Somerset.

The story concluded as Paul leant over the rail, again. This time the sea-gods took pity and Paul was blessed with a momentary treasure of happiness. He caught a beautiful gurnard, only to see it leap out his hands back into a balmy sea as he held it up for me to take a photo. All he could muster at the plop was a quiet "oh".

With Neptune so whimsical, Paul became inconsolable, and not a further fish was hooked by any of us. Further tugs and tangles revealed only hook impaled sea anemones, the varieties of which could only have been identified by Burnham born marine biologist Thomas Alan Stephenson, a world specialist in those small, tentacled, rock-sucking wobble-blobs.

When Martin accidentally spilt hot tea over Paul's lap, it was clear that he was already a broken man, looking as sad as the gull-poo stained statue of the Ancient Mariner on Watchet promenade. Indeed, he had to suffer for several hours more, changing colour like a chameleon, staring overboard at fulmars morphing into albatross. The only sounds where sploshes and the snapping of Dave-the-Graphic's camera as a pair of gannets dived beside the boat seeking the live bait on Honest John's hook. Samuel Taylor Coleridge captured the torpor:

'We stuck, nor breath nor motion;
As idle as a painted ship
Upon a painted ocean.'

Such a state can infect one with a fever of mind. As Fleetwood Mac entered Big Jeremy's through his iPod, Weston's favourite son, John Cleese, entered mine as I chomped listlessly on a rich tea biscuit. J.C. dragged things out in blonde wig, blue skirt and pinafore as an usherette, selling dead albatross in the infamous Monty Python cinema sketch. "What flavour is it?" he shouts. "It's a bird. It's a

TWIN HULLS & HOOF GLUE

bloody seabird. It's not any bloody flavour ...Gannet on a stick."
Molly, I knew, would not have approved.

Vagrant from the Tristan da Cunha Islands and utterly lost, Molly
was a two-year old Atlantic Yellow-nosed Albatross, or Thalassarche
chlororhynchus to those appreciating detail, and, like Ray's sand-
eels, had been found on Burnham beach. And a rare touchdown it
was, too. Being oceanic birds albatross seldom venture near to
shore. According to *Bird International* the only two previously
accepted accounts of yellow-nosed albatross sighted within an area
covering Europe and North Africa was one in 1985 off the coast of
Cornwall and one in 1994 in Norway, and both those historic birds
were well out to sea at the time. Molly turned up at the end of June
2007.

Her segmented beak gave her an almost prehistoric look. However,
it lacked the distinctive golden stripe along the top of the bill attained
in adulthood. Molly was a youngster to those in the know. As a whole
she was achingly beautiful. Somerset was either blessed or damned,
either way the cross-bolt shooting Ancient Mariner and J.C. should
rightly feel ashamed. Home was south across Brent Knoll, and the M5,
and over six thousand miles away. These facts may well have
distressed her. Hordes of click-click-clicketing twitchers, however,
would probably have upset her more, judging by the pained cries
above and alongside us, as Dave-the-Graphic continued to fire away
like a turret gunner of Her Majesty's navy.

Wrapped in a towel by her local saviours, Hugh and Pauline Harris,
Molly was smuggled into 'Secret World', a nearby animal sanctuary
where wildlife cameraman Simon King filmed caged owls against a
black painted tarpaulin backdrop and a folly brick chimney-stack, and
where one can also hire a bicycle. With Molly being neither owl nor
ET, administrator Simon Kinder, decided upon her having a good
night's rest before a Brean Down early morning release. All albatross
are clumsy on the ground and need a headwind or an exposed cliff-
edge site to take off.

The writer Ralph Whitlock thought the Down "looms like a
mountain and thrusts out into the Channel like the Rock of Gibraltar."
Indeed, the 200-feet high limestone promontory, used as a location
for filming the TV drama 'Bone Kickers' and popular with enthusiastic
model aeroplane flyers, was ideal for a sky seeking albatross. Away on
the wind without GPS connection or compass prior to the arrival of
any twirling propeller, Molly was spotted a day later off Sweden. Long
before her Burnham adventure had been picked up by BBC Points
West and angry twitcher blogs began. It is reassuring to know that she

will be protected wherever she glides. Yellow-nosed albatross are regarded as endangered, threatened by long-line fishing. On board the *Gemini*, baited hooks on short traces seemed not to be endangering anything.

Agreed, for a minute or two Mike-the-Trike did endanger himself, swearing that chain mail gloves should be obtainable by prescription on the NHS. He had cut deep into his thumb while pollack gutting. Seeing the blood of man meld with that of fish, he begged Ray's superglue to bond the wound together. It did the job.

Ray patted his tackle box and torpor resumed, only relieved when Big Jeremy made the deduction that a female ling roe, cut by Ray from the biggest catch of the day, resembled an extra large flaccid phallus. This insight gave me a moment of clarity as to why a roe deer gaining its first antlers is called a pricket. It was also an invitation for Ray, having now settled on a ling being a condonger, to pose for lewd camera snaps until the distraction embarrassed intelligence. Our joint behaviour, like Molly, was immature.

As *Gemini's* engines finally gunned for home with Mick hosing away the day's gore and slime, I was reminded of Yank humourist, Dave Barry's observation that "Fishing is boring, unless you catch an actual fish, and then it is disgusting." Everybody's welcome to their opinion.

Back on shore, Honest John sang a verse or two of 'Jerusalem', and Paul swore to stick to his own little boat in Watchet, despite complaints ad nauseam about Hinkley B and the polluted Severn Sea. Aboard the *Gemini*, there was going to be room for another. Perhaps even two, if I didn't fork out on a rod of value. Where to go other than Highbridge? Beside a very new roundabout is the dank darkness of 'Thyers', a sea fisherman's Elysium where live bait wriggles and writhes in shop counter display tubs. As it was Honest John's favourite pit they surely would have a bargain boat-rod and lures of cunning.

For me, the day's memory was to linger. A month later my car boot still had a niff of microbial fermentation, when Honest John made one of that evening's obligatory phone calls

"Ray, you on for tomorrow?"

"What's tomorrow?"

"First Sunday in the month. It's fishing, Ray."

"Oh, oh, oh. But I can't come!"

"So, see you on the next first one."

"What's then?"

"It's fishing, Ray!"

"Oh, oh, oh."

## TAINDIK
# WHIFF OF ORCHIDS

*"Part of the secret of success in life is to eat what you like and let the food fight it out inside."*

Mark Twain (American Humourist, and Writer, 1835-1910)

There is a saying, "when two friends understand each other totally, the words are soft and strong like an orchid's perfume." Like my wife, and having spent some time in Thailand documentary film-making, I had developed an attachment to orchids. Adorning many a pavement café, their purple blooms brightened grubby Bangkok streets, and their pungent fragrance permeated the carbon excretions.

Closer to home, Writhlington School in Radstock, in addition to being named the most enterprising school in England, is famous for its orchid collection and its links with Brazil, Costa Rica and Guatemala. Indeed the school houses the biggest collection of orchids outside Kew Gardens. This said, Somerset also delights in having various wild orchids, or 'granfer griggles' as some call them. One of these is very special, being one of the rarest and endangered plants in Britain. After a botanist friend told me where they grew, curiosity had got the Berrow sand "allus a-shiften and a-blowen" in my boots.

With warblers calling out 'a-tak-tak-tak' in early May sunshine, I was very careful where I put my feet as I looked in the dunes for any sign of lizard orchids. Each plant has up to a hundred and fifty lizard-like greenish-purple flowers that have an overpoweringly rustic whiff of goat. My fishing companion friend Ray had imparted his extensive botanical knowledge to me about it.

"A most attractive flower, orchis hircinum," he confided, "exuding an unfortunate pong, unless you're a Billy. I cannot imagine what benefit this may confer upon the plant. Maybe something to do with goatal dissemination? Maybe it makes Billy ripe for rumpy-pumpy. Reproduction can be fascinating. The seeds are incredibly light, very like fern spores, and are not in fact 'seeds' as we usually understand them. This could make a serious 'O' level subject I suspect.

"I do know that many tropical orchids depend on the flower resembling another insect to attract pollination. Perhaps these are slowly evolving to one day look like a goat? A three foot stinking, horned and bearded shaggy orchid might be all the rage in distant times to come."

Ray was always so very contemplative.

However, my caution was not through fear of stepping on floral charm, but because down the road, Alan Wakeley, a local postman, had been bitten on the hand by something more definitely reptilian. True, the adder was in Brean Cove post box at the time, and probably seeing red from the occasional dropping postcard, but I felt my trepidation justified. After blowing a fork-tongued raspberry, the snake had 'taken off'. But where? Doubling back, across the National Trust car park, there was safety in the high ground. Straight ahead, a few desultory cattle and sandy tarmac might have seemed as good an option. But then, oh my goodness, there would have come a surprise – the gaudy lights of hell's half mile. 'Grockleshell City'. Here Pontins, Stardust, Brean Leisure Park and Bunnies Supermarket cater for the Black Country chip-butty legions stomping out from rented regimented boxes of tin. A loose narked adder among that lot didn't bear thinking about. Thankfully, Alan the postie was okay.

An adder bite is comparable in discomfort to a bad dumbledore sting. Consequently, Alan, being made of stoic, had been happy to suck the venom from the deep puncture marks himself. No great harm was done. Yet, despite this, the offending post box had been closed as a precaution. This added to local snail-mailing problems that extended to the muddy Parrett from a spate of post box thefts using a spade, or failing that, an oxycetalyne cutter.

In the village of Mudgely all that was left was a hole in the ground. And in East Huntspill, a local resident was incredulous, telling local television news that he had "heard of postal cuts, but this is ridiculous. Who would want to steal a post box? It's very inconvenient."

When the BBC asked the police why it was happening, an inspector spoke into the microphone surmising that "it's probably memorabilia value." Adding, just to make the mind of villain tick, "They can fetch between £200 and £400."

Berrow nature reserve meanwhile was an oasis of calm, even with a female community police officer browsing in gorse bushes. Having searched a goodly while myself the only curiosities I found were a gnarled sand-rooted apple tree in full blossom beside a clump of teasels and vibrant coloured chemical stains from Ragwort control.

So I gave up on petalled and slithering lizard, instead turning my attention to discovering a 'lost' relative of a new friend, Robert Cave. I thought it would be nice to help. This was a man who had got the West Country bug, like myself, from a tender age, ever since his mother moved down from London to become a horse handler, and be near family – much of which, I gathered, was 'well heeled' and fairly elusive. Some vanished as missionaries to China and all that remained of them were names burnt into document boxes. And a scribbled note in pencil from the Queen of Portugal, that Robert had chanced upon on e-bay, wanted to 'ascertain' where a certain Lady Cave, an artist obsessed with drawing ants, had got to. So knowing the exact whereabouts of any relation was a bonus.

My Berrow search followed a chat with Robert during Thai New Year 2552 as the multitudes of croci in Dulverton churchyard, in that Exmoor jodhpur town, were giving up the ghost, drooping their jaded heads on rice noodle stems. A day when Sondhi Limthongkul, the leader of Thailand's yellow-shirted protest movement was shot and hurt in Bangkok in an apparent assassination attempt.

The event bore heavily on the mind. So, unsurprisingly my duck was instinctive when a shout of 'four!' meant I could legally be hit on the head. Between the dead and the sea, Berrow clubbers are easily distracted by the rare possibility of big birdies. Perhaps even the odd albatross and eagle. Warning signs seem pinned to every available gatepost, and I paraphrase, 'Sod off. You can't park here. This is private property 'cos we're all golfers.' Unlike myself, at least the lizard orchid should be grateful. Until hackers began slicing about the rough during the 1980s, there were a few hundred Lizard Orchids within our shores, now there are reportedly thousands. Why? Well, the golfers tended to brush the pollen with their designer kit, moist with dew and tears, and the dust-like seeds stuck to be transferred to other areas. It also explains why there's the peculiar whiff of goat about at local cocktail parties in spring.

Protected by a high stone bramble-shrouded wall from miscued hard hitting spheres unleashed by the orchid saviours, 'Great Uncle George' lay beneath sandy molehills, and yellow kingcups, kicking up the daisies with his wife Estella.

He had not been totally forgotten, which I felt could easily happen judging by many a toppled churchyard cross close by. Someone had put a posy of fresh exotic flowers on the grave. It was a touch of class probably met with spirited approval. Great Uncle George after all, was a Viscount. The large granite gravestone discoloured with yellow lichen denoted a man apart. Chiselled words read:

'George Cave of Richmond, GCMG, Lord High Chancellor of Great Britain 1922-1924, 1924-1928. Chancellor of Oxford University 1925-1928. Born 1856. Died 1928. A man who neither sought or shunned greatness but found it in the path of duty.'

Lacking space because of big lettering, the memorial omits to say that 'Old Uncle George' was Home Secretary under David Lloyd George during the last two years of the First World War, as well as being the MP for Barnstaple. Choosing Somerset for his eternity he possibly shared the same misgivings about Devonian soil as the majority of Summerlanders.

He was also created an earl. That day should have been one of cele-bration. It wasn't, he died within hours. Perhaps, it was the shock. Instead, Estella was created Countess Cave of Richmond. Having had no children, the viscountcy became extinct when he snuffed it. The earldom, likewise, when Estella left the mortal coil. The couple had good innings, which is perhaps just as well. The family motto's 'Cave Deus Videt', beware, God sees.

Standing alone in the midday sun, I thought the family crest looked a trifle dog-eared. Four deerhounds, as well as a rampant stag, were upon it. Oh, a hunting lot, I thought. Compelled to ask, "Mad dogs of Englishmen?" I wanted put the question to Robert, who compared to the Viscount, couldn't be more different. But doing himself down as being "bit of a duffer" and "having problems with nerves", Robert is unkind on himself. The footsteps of politicians are not the most advisable ones to follow.

The detection of Great Uncle George's resting place, however, had so impressed Robert that I got an invite to a celebratory Dulverton lunch. Knowing what the cuisine would be, my acceptance was immediate. It would be like old times. Venison was definitely not on the menu, the rampant stag on the Cave family crest being merely a circumstantial connection to Exmoor. Robert's passion was towards Asia.

Stood at the bar of 'Tongdam Thai Restaurant', co-owned with his business partner Tino from Thailand's famous Chatree Gold Mining area, Robert looked dapper. A white-haired clean-shaven sophisticate in a long-sleeved, blue-striped, Saville Row shirt, he had conceded to informality with jeans and trainers. To look at him, there was little resemblance to the bronze bust of the man in a lawyer's long wig, prominent bushy eyebrows, moustache and lace cravat sculpted by Lady Désirée Welby that sits today in Oxford University. More so when Old Uncle George had the Orders of St Michael and St George, while Robert took the orders of Gaeng Phed Ped Yang and Pla Rard Prik. Outside, under an ancient grape vine was a Thai purple orchid in rude health. This I understood was where Robert 'goes floppy as a crocus'. Fortnightly, unwinding under an Exmoor sky, a glass of wine in hand after a couple of hundred mile trip from London, car seats and boot filled with blanket-covered ice boxes of fresh supplies. For me, it was well worth the effort. Emanating cooking aromas were a wonderful tug back to Bangkok.

After sitting ourselves at a table, Robert appeared slightly distracted placing his mobile by his napkin. As soon as he did so, a tune played. It was Tino saying he had ticked all the right boxes and had been granted a British passport. Robert was ecstatic. Set against this good news, two new Thai staff were still being 'processed' and a retired local school teacher was on standby to drum English into their heads. The ever-changing goalposts of the Government's new visa regulations made matters very difficult. Now everything has to be paid for up front and corruption was not just rife in Thailand. Agencies are seizing the opportunity to open up offering 'guaranteed' passes in exchange for hefty fee.

So, it's a community effort in Dulverton to keep Tongdam straight. June Day, for example, was once a previous owner. Back then, Tongdam was a shop with a forte in antiques, not food. June, though, cannot shed her attachment, still helps out everyday as an invaluable general factotum. Accounts, Robert and Tino admit, are not their strongpoint.

Knowing of Tino's achievement made Robert visibly more relaxed. Enough to reveal more ancestral history. When Great Uncle George was forty, another old relative, Basil Silitto Cave, became an overnight embarrassment taking the flak for causing the shortest war in world history that lasted thirty-eight minutes over an impasse about a flag. In a run-of-the-mill bit of Empire meddling, Basil, the British Consul and Diplomatic Agent to Zanzibar, apparently chose the wrong man to be sultan in the opinion of the sultan's nephew who had gone ahead and appointed himself. Both men refused to change their minds, with the nephew, Khalid bin Bargash, flying a flag above the palace as a sign of his dissidence.

On 27th August 1896, Khalid declared that "We have no intention of hauling down our flag and we do not believe you would open fire on us." To which Basil replied, "We do not want to open fire, but unless you do as you are told, we shall certainly do so." And, two British warships did. Five hundred people died, mostly from a fire in the palace. A British sailor suffered injury from paltry retaliation, but later got better in hospital. A Reuters news correspondent reported that Khalid had "fled at the first shot." So in Basil's book, Britain won. Unfortunately, the naval guns also inadvertently destroyed the German consulate, which wasn't very helpful in years to come.

Best to change the subject, I thought. On the menu was durian cheesecake. In its raw state on a tree a durian fruit looks like a giant horse chestnut, a conker with exaggerated clout. A falling fruit hit a man on the head in his own back garden, killing him. So repulsive is the flesh that the pong makes the smell of a Lizard orchid pale into insignificance. Thais nickname durian 'stinky fruit' and ban it from public transport and hotels. In ignorance my wife took a single durian as a gift wrapped in plastic bags on a two-hour bus journey across Bangkok during which passengers began gagging. "Oh look, you've got durian," I said.

"Just a little something I picked up," Robert replied. Thankfully fate had previously allowed him to pick up something of more merit. For two years he had sold antiques from a stall in London's Portobello Road. Of course, I thought, trying to piece together the Tongdam jigsaw in my head, that must be why he got on so well with June. Anyway, one day he was shown a piece of Chinese silver adorned with an exquisite and intricate bee. At the time this was the most beautiful object he had ever seen, and enough to make him a collector of Chinese silver ever since.

The best way to find more of the same was to travel, and his uncertain road began. Needing money to eat in Hong Kong led him to be an extra 'on the cutting room floor' in 'Shanghai Surprise.' A very bad film, he thought, despite starring Sean Penn. Undaunted, he gave acting another go and tried for the role of a Hong Kong boat captain in the TV film 'China Hand', hoping to play alongside David Soul. Sadly, learning lines by rote was a mistake. His mind went a blank at the screen test. Malaysia, Singapore, and Thailand, and every other place one might care to mention in the Far East, brought better fortune and with it came the seed of idea of opening an East-meets-

West style of restaurant that was to blossom into Tongdam. A small corner and courtyard in Dulverton became the fulfilment of his life's ambition.

The atmosphere is immediately welcoming. A place of character. Never did Robert want a 'Little Thailand' when the shutters closed. Yes, Thai news arrives by satellite reporting a country now in disrepair, particularly in the south near the border with Malaysia. Atrocities are happening there that go unreported in the west. Disturbing stuff that distresses Robert as much the staff that are like his family, and who are all integrated into the town. Indeed, Thais had connections with the West Country even in Great Uncle George's time.

Prince Chula of Siam, for instance, owned a country mansion set in a peaceful valley, and was legal guardian of Prince Bira, a famous motor racing champion of the 1930s and 1940s with a team called 'White Mouse Racing.' Hard to imagine Bira in his Riley Imp, though, keeping pace with Frome's favourite son, Jenson Button.

Joh, Tongdam's head waiter, shows off his sporting talent with a cue. Cherry picked from a famous Bangkok restaurant and a modern stalwart of the local pub pool team, he whispered urgently into Robert's ear.

"Oh dear, there's trouble in the kitchen. Want to meet Heng?" Robert said.

"Love to," I said. Chef Heng was a local legend. Each morning he became the bane of the Co-op, policing the shelves, furiously pointing at sell-by dates and demanding discounts. The supermarket always seemed busier when word got out that Heng was doing his shopping.

Animated in his spotless food prep area, Heng was not a happy man. Whitecoated, hair under a blue elasticated plastic cap and wearing oversized yellow rubber gloves, he waved a 'touting' letter from 'Gordon Ramsey's Kitchen Nightmares' production company Optomen Television. "I do not need Mr Ramsey in my kitchen!" Heng shouted. He had every right to be angry. Tongdam had been awarded five stars for hygiene after an impromptu visit from the inspectorate at a time when Joh and Heng were 'holding the fort'.

"It's okay, Heng," soothed Robert. "They're just canvassing the willing."

Behind us, the restaurant had become extremely busy with adjacent tables filled by 'ladies who lunch.' These are nostalgic gatherings of a dying breed. Quintessentially English in prim floral dresses; powder-nosed, they speak 'properly' through pursed lips about their memories of Singapore and India when they were 'gals.' Among them was Mrs Stanbury, a beneficiary of a Burmese childhood and these days the owner of Dulverton's principal garage. Should the need arise 'to go the bathroom', none are short in coming forward. The loo is an eccentric relic, sitting in a dark recess beyond a cast iron bath where walls of peeling wallpaper are decorated with glued-on crisp bronzed leaves of autumn. Apparently the ladies love it.

Quiet conversing mentions in passing Nasi Goreng. Nothing to do with war, of course. The dish of rice, onion and egg cooked specially by Heng was Robert's favourite and 'off menu'. Realising early on that West Somerset represents all things best of a fading England, Robert has found his market niche. Tongdam is an ex-pat's paradise. A genteel club not given to the sign language of Berrow.

Possibly due to Robert's eye for detail put down to also owning a packaging company in London, collected artefacts are carefully arranged in cabinets, while artworks from the Far East hang from the white walls. The exceptions are two paintings from Japan. These are propped up on a mantelpiece after the Exmoor damp rusted away their hanging nails.

A large watercolour of a Chinese street scene is a favourite of a regular diner known locally as 'Thai John', who always eats his meals gazing into the picture at the noodle sellers and washerwomen of a hundred years ago. Reclusive, and a walking *Encyclopedia Britannica*, Thai John lives in a tiny cottage shared with a phenomenal amount of books and without television, down a long narrow overgrown track on the outskirts of town.

During the cricket season, Test Match Special radio commentary floats through an open window to entertain attentive wildlife. Even in isolation, he is a man who still dresses for dinner in the civilised manner adopted in bygone days living for many years in a teak house in colonial Bangkok. Rumour has it that the look of wistful nostalgia that overcame him when showed a photograph that Robert had taken during a recent Thailand visit defied description. Defying the odds, Thai John's house remains standing today, draped with electrical spaghetti, and dwarfed by the pollution-stained immensity of high-rise. A survivor.

Similar to 'Thai John' is 'Army John'. A retired officer from the Burma campaign he, like Robert boasts an accomplished uncle. Montague Russell Page, was considered to be the foremost landscape architect of his time. Empathetic to the traditions of European and Islamic gardening he could have been a blessing to Zanzibar. Partnered by Geoffrey Jellicoe and imagining a gateway to the under-world, he designed the landscape and iconic modernist 'Caveman

Restaurant' building at Cheddar Gorge.

Before his death in 1985 Montague had clients that included the Duke and Duchess of Windsor, King Léopold III of the Belgians and PepsiCo. The essence of Montague is best captured in his own words: "Whether I am making a landscape or a garden or arranging a window-box, I first address the problem as an artist composing a picture." This is as true for Robert. There are many Thai restaurants in Somerset, but surely none can match the Tongdam's mellow cultural ambience in which everything is 'just so'.

Happiness, he discovered a long while ago, goes through the tummy. That recipe is something very special and all to do with having Exmoor Thais.

As I bade my farewells, having declined the kind offer of cheese-cake, I couldn't help thinking whether the Thai purple orchid under the vine was real or silk? Well, that was something to discover another time in the not too distant future. Either way, at least it wouldn't reek of goat.

## TOTHERYDIK
# MOOSEMAN & PUDDING STONE

*"If nature were not beautiful, it would not be worth knowing, and if nature were not worth knowing, life would not be worth living."*

Henri Poincaré (French physicist 1854-1912)

The headline story in the *Bridgwater Mercury* read 'Burnham all set for Baywatch stars'. Perhaps someone in the news room had remembered the French and Saunders Baywatch sketch filmed on Berrow Beach in 1996. Anyway, it was April Fool's day, and possibly the hottest day of the year so far. But too warm for an overcoat? I wasn't sure. So I grabbed my worn-pocketed thick Moldovan and went outside to wait.

I had imagined spending the morning with 'Mousseman', having once experienced a devil in the kitchen with a beer in his hand. I was proved mistaken, soon deducing that it was 'Mooseman' by a life-size plastic, inflated 'made in China' moose head sharing space with a chainsaw in the back of a 4x4 pick-up that arrived outside my blue front gate. Knowing my curiosity of where my ancient garden cobbles came from, Mooseman had offered to show me a hush-hush place a rook's flight away where he had built a shed. But I wasn't to say where. Things get repeated. There was some problem, I understood, with planning permission.

All I was interested in, I assured, was his puddings ... and why Mooseman?

Explanation was reluctant. The nickname was his brother's fault, who began calling his sibling 'Musso' after realising he thought about sex every five seconds like Mussolini, the small Italian dictator with a big ego. Musso got corrupted to 'Moose', and then into 'Mooseman'. Unlike Mussolini, Mooseman was just big, with shaggy grey hair, stubbled cheeks, a hint of moustache, and Basset hound eyes. And what a gene pool. A cross between Russian/German ballerina and English/Irish wordsmith.

His father, a notable poet, once wrote poetry for pints, fished to pay the rent, and was a friend to both Dylan Thomas and Francis Bacon. Fifty years ago, deep in a wood, both Mooseman and his brother grew up in a fifteenth century gamekeeper's thatched cottage, peppercorn rented from a poetry-loving landowner. Filled by memories of walls yellowed by tobacco, cricket on the dicky transistor, and 'a clutter that seemed blown in from some magical otherness', Mooseman believes his childhood made him the man he is – one of Nature's romantics. What I perceived was a gentle man led by Roselle Angwin's verse "How might we step on the earth's thin skin if not by treading lightly." He's a clever bugger, artistically talented and inheriting, folk say, his dad's mischievous smile of eternal youth, although I couldn't vouch for maternal calluses on his toes.

Being a carpetbagger of sorts, impishness made him happy and it showed in his latest project. Unsurprisingly, it was in a wood, one that Mooseman bought a few years ago, for the price of a couple of ropey second hand cars, to become ten acres of sloping solace. Nothing is perfect, however. Methods in modern farming have made his spring water undrinkable because of leeching nitrates. Sad, but still the trickles keep his hands clean.

A service tree and a spindle were giveaways that his Somerset woodland is ancient. Amongst such maturity, he had added a new arrival, a baby Christmas tree. "My family and I are going to spend Christmases here," he said softly. A woodland solstice to rekindle the past, creating cherished memories for the future. His three children were blessed.

From beside the infant tree I gawped at Mooseman's 'shed', as yet unfinished, lovingly made of timber and cadged recyclables that even included a set of patio doors. He had been the master of understatement. With more space than the Victorian semi-detached that was his official home, this was a cabin exuding permanence,

Now he was cultivating the camouflage. For insulation, old carpet had been rolled out on top of the flat roof. In turn, the intention was to cover this in a layer of soil seeded with Creeping Red Fescue, a hardy grass that does was the name suggests. Under leaf shade it would grow to about an inch, ideal for the gentle scything of a grass commonly used on airfields. Ah, Mooseman and scythe, I thought, what a wonderful photo opportunity for a snapshot of life in rural Somerset. A better one offered itself as we spied a small plane, buzzing overhead. Mooseman became frantic in scooping up clods of soil in his ample hands, scattering hope of sodding the Axminster. He didn't want the pilot getting any ideas.

As plane noise slowly became as distant as the far sound of traffic, Mooseman visibly relaxed. But I understood him. An artist needs somewhere to work and for a man who had created acclaimed public art from Cambridge to Tintagel, this was his private place. "Bigger than a caravan," he conceded. "If things go tits up in life I've got a hermitage."

"Don't go the same way as Duncan," I said, recalling the hermit who lived in a wooden chalet at Dunster Beach for years. "He died a few months ago, something that went unnoticed for ages."

And so we chatted, Mooseman and I, in his timeless place beneath buzzard mews and the pig-like grunts of a raven. Genial conversation was cushion-comfy, our feet on the veranda rail. Ah, the rail. Amazing how a ballerina gene could surface.

"Is that an art installation?" I said, nodding my head in the direction of an unwholesome looking lump squatting on a corner seat.

"No, it's earth oven sour dough bread made in Tracebridge and it's defrosting for breakfast."

This was a man who knew his colley from his coley, and his chicken-in-the-wood from his tree-rabbit. I spoke of living life by cat miaows and awaiting rare letters from Afghanistan where Lawrence, my eldest, had army work reporting desert movements of the Taliban. Mooseman listened, his mind cogs turning. "So when you go for a jobs description at the careers office after school and say, 'I'd like to be a Taliban Teller. A Teller of the Taliban, please.' do they reply 'Oh, we've got a nice one for you in Afghanistan'?"

I winced. "My lad thought TT racing was something completely different."

There was a light thud and drifting of a small feather. Below us a chaffinch blinked. Dazed. Mooseman sighed. "That's a pity, that pane of glass wasn't there yesterday. Probably best it was just a pink-twink, a badger would have been shattering blow."

Looking up at an aged oak tree just in front of us, he continued. "An old boy hereabouts used to say, 'I know what we'll do. We'll get a brick and chuck him up in the air and if he do come down, we got to go to work, and if he stop up there, we got to have a day off.' Well, I chucked a brick of my own up there eight years ago, but best move now, the kettle's boiling." And so it was, blackened on a sooted sheet of metal, resting on bricks, over a small fire-pit dug into red soil a few yards away. As well as a cup of Earl Grey, Mooseman could make a great chapatti.

The rising smoke was sunshine caught and reflected by a large, round 'Claude mirror', the invention of the great landscape painter Claude Lorraine, who came up with the idea of putting glass on location. Coated with a black substance on the back it reflected the image behind you. Basically he framed his landscape. It works. Instead of looking at everything around, that can be just too much to take in, you could actually see what you were painting. Rather like the way an artist used a wooden frame with string as a boxed image.

Leant against an ash that had violets flowering in a tree-fork, Mooseman's mirror looked a bit slug eaten and I remarked on it.

"Oh, at some point I'll give it some TLC and put it somewhere, I don't know where. I have lots of things to put."

I could see that. A camera obscura, another artist's aid, sat on a sawn tree stump. He had been playing around with camera obscuras since the solar eclipse of 1999, which inspired his 'first dabblings'. The one misty in kettle steam had been meant for Weston-super-Mare with the idea of having hundreds in a circle like a rose window. However, they would never have been admired. Nobody told Mooseman that the whole shebang was destined for a lecture theatre that had, because of the acoustics, wall to ceiling draped curtains.

"In most of my work I have to give people ideas and plans and with this sort of stuff I can change my mind in a second." He pointed at an ash tree trimmed of its limbs save for a growing twiglet growing from the trunk. "This was going to be a tree with steps up it and a seat on top, but it didn't. It became more.

A place starts speaking to you. A place is dark. You come in with one idea and as you start working on it, the space becomes lighter and gives you other ideas where to take it.

The work is completely governed by the seasons, so I do a lot of my work in winter when trees aren't producing sap."

His brick in the tree could feasibly stay until autumn.

Beside the camera obscura, a green door, numbered with a one, rotted and an old copper lay upturned in the ivy. He had brought both from home after a clear out. People used to do the week's washing in the copper, when it used to have a wooden surround and space underneath, where a fire was lit. In would go the water and that would be the week's washing. Living in a row of four houses, Mooseman's was the one where everyone would come to do their ablutions. Now it was in the wood because, like the door, the magpie in him wanted the copper kept.

And the same went for a moss-covered go-cart of rope, planks and pram wheels. A mental image of Mooseman careering down through the wood roaring, "Mooo-oooh-aaah!" gave me an involuntary twitch.

He put down his empty tea mug. "Right, pudding time. Let's go for a walk. First stop, the badger setts." Seems a trifle optimistic, I thought.

Indeed, we halted in moments to admire where trees had been shrigged and shrowded, that's to say trimmed and lopped. Something Mooseman does a lot when clearing a 'sight line' – a wide path to the layman – in a crush of harts-tongue ferns and dog's mercury, which is an odd name, given perhaps because it's poisonous. Or does it give a mutt a mercurial tongue? Here and there intricately carved sculptures with names like 'Jailer's Lament' and 'Witch's Topiary' had been strategically placed to catch the observant eye.

Somewhere from among the trees came rapid drumming. "Rain-pie." he said.

"What?"

"Rain-pie. The old word for woodpecker."

"Why?"

Mooseman shrugged. "Dunno. Soggy pastry? Or wishful thinking, when people cut a crust. Perhaps woodpecker meat's very dry and folk asked for succulence. On the other hand, rarity must have made the pie irritatingly noisy."

I queried what his favourite birdy word was and he answered without a moment's thought, "Titty-todger." On the cusp of asking why a wren should be called this, I refrained. This was Mooseman, after all. Anyway, we had to get on.

As early dumbledores, wasps and hornets buzzed without bearings, I, too, followed the teaching of Angwin, careful not to tread on prim-roses, violets and stichwort, and aware that the first flowers of English bluebells were beginning to show. Scrunching on an abundance of pungent wild garlic, however, was unavoidable. Brambles drew blood, stinging nettles, a relative of elm in the plant kingdom believe it or not, met their job description; and rabbit holes were traps.

A small skull caused Mooseman to bend and pick up. "Rat? Um. Probably tree-rabbit," he said with conviction. "Only the saddle and hind legs are worth eating." Personally speaking, I had never tried squirrel, so I couldn't comment. Squirrels were much more useful, along with jays and crows, as absent-minded conservationists. Many a Somerset oak tree resulted from a forgotten buried acorn stash.

"There was a skeleton of deer here once," said Mooseman, still on his subject. "Most likely got hit by car and dragged itself into the wood to die. I watched the carcass slowly fall apart and disappear as animals dragged bits away."

It was tough going for me as well. Snow had brought trees down across the paths leaving enough room for badgers to pass beneath them, but not a Mooseman or Chazzer. On the bark of a toppled thin ash we both noticed peculiar black fungal growths, the size of half ping-pong balls. "Oooh, King Alfred's cakes," Mooseman said.

Here in a name was a reminder of an ancient Somerset anonymously immortalised by quill in the *Life of Saint Neot* over a thousand years ago. As Alfred languished over cooking-fire incinerations among the Athelney reed beds, he got a proper telling off from the wife of Denewulf, for being understandably distracted by other responsibilities.

"Cas'n the mind the ke-aks, man, an' doosen zee 'em burn. I'm boun thee's eat 'em vast enough, az zoon az tiz the turn."

If words can be believed, in a toss up between facing that hut-wife and the irritating Danes, the latter probably felt the preferable option for Alfred. Oh, wonderfulness, buns were to make England great.

"You'll like this," said Mooseman, taking a penknife from his pocket. Cutting a canker from the tree, he carefully sliced off the bottom to reveal a pattern of black and white rings. Such prettiness. "There. If you put it out by the fire at home it'll dry out and be as beautiful as beautiful." Also called 'ash cankers' the fungus only grows on ash trees, as the name implies.

Eventually, with me sun-sweated inside my daft overcoat impulse, we stopped by a 'cave', a sett long disused. Had Mooseman seen many badgers in his wood? "No. Despite sitting as quiet as a church mouse, not a sausage."

Badger evidence though was clear enough. And their digging services deserved peanut payments. Scuffled out the 'cave' entrance were cobbles, just like the ones outside my warped blue front door, denoting badgers with middle-class taste. This was pudding country and all about us were the weirdest of rocky outcrops.

Watching me scrutinise a lump that was about five foot high and nine foot long, Mooseman gave it a pat and announced it was called 'breccia'. We were standing in an old cobble quarry. The cobbles were in the breccia, he explained, a conglomerate of hard stuff formed during the Ice Age. Glaciers pushed mud, pebbles and stones down through Britain. During the slow abrasive journey pebbles and stones were rolled, smoothed and rounded to become cobbles. Where the bulk came to rest the mud hardened forming cement that held things together. Geological bods could have named the mixture 'rock cake'. Instead, they chose the cosier 'pudding stone', suggesting an idyll of cuddles and warmth.

There were numerous seams of pudding in the area. To have found outcrops in his wood, Mooseman thought fantastic. Many a quaint courtyard and pathway lay as yet untapped. He especially liked the holes made where cobbles had fallen out. Summering martins spying potential nesting holes would get a shock, however.

"Whooomph ... booow!" he laughed.

There had to be one last question. In all the wood, what was his favourite thing? "At the moment? The clump of violets growing in the ash tree," he said. For that sensitivity alone Mooseman deserved to remain incognito.

Later, when my youngest son Felix came home from his Starbuck's shift, he itched to tell the story of students scribbling illegibly and pouring coffee over themselves after reading the European Union was insisting that Taunton people become left handed as part of an experiment.

The local paper reported the plans were opposed by Bob Wright, a man prepared to go to prison in a stand for right-handedness. However, the European Equality Commission's Mano Izquierda was adamant the initiative would go ahead with the support of Paolo Fril, the European Commissioner for Left-Handedness.

Apparently, Felix asked the gullibles if they knew a bit of Spanish or did any anagrams.

It was that kind of day. At the end of which, by the fire, my King Alfred's cake became as beautiful as beautiful.

## Recipe for Mooseman Nettle Soup

Serves two, or one if enthusiastic.

1 x pair thick gloves
3 x handful of washed stinging nettle tips
1 x medium-sized onion or a few shallots chopped
1 x knob of butter
1 x tablespoon of grapeseed oil
   450 ml water
   Salt
1 x slice of bread cut into cubes

Putting on a pair gloves pick the nettle tips. Heat butter in a heavy pan over a medium heat then add the chopped onion or shallots and sweat. When transparent throw in the nettle tips and stir for two minutes. Add the water and simmer for about twenty-five minutes. Salt to taste. Liquidise and keep warm. Using a frying pan heat the oil. Add the bread and fry, turning once, to make croutons. Pour soup into bowls and serve with the croutons on top. Cheap, nutritious and eccentric.

## FOTHERYDIK
# PLANET PATRICK

*"Invention, it must be humbly admitted, does not consist of creating out of void, but out of chaos."*

Mary Wollstonecraft Shelley (Romantic Novelist, 1797-1851)

Mid-March, and I was listening to jargon often described in the 'Bearin' Up' as " highly testicle".

"Nought-point-five percent. The lowest interest rate ever" crackled the distortion of radio noise. On a day of in-and-out sunshine Somerset was to hold hands with neighbours and, with the jingle-joy of a Morris dancer, take a leap into the dark. The Bank of England was to make new money by tapping figures into cyber space in exchange for assets. This would give intangible squillions to banks so that pinstriped wallahs could lend to small business. I scratched head. It was not real money like the valued crumpled stuff in an honesty box, just make belief stuff. Or was I missing something? Interest in my cat's rainy day fund was shrinking, shrinking.

The news hadn't helped my sombre mood on a day with my eldest son only days away from donning his battle fatigues and leaving for desert heat. The situation had become grave in Taunton town centre. Horn honking frustration, caused by traffic lights stopped on red, quietened to irreverent peeps. As the reason explained itself, even the peepers berated themselves, stilling engines, subdued in wait. A funeral cortege of over a hundred motor-bikers, a company of grieving friends, preceded a hearse bearing a coffin draped in the Union

Jack topped with a soldier's cap. Corporal Tom Gaden, a Somerset rifleman, had come home from Afghanistan.

I needed an antidote, somewhere other-worldly, although I wasn't about to cross the Levels to Wincanton, where streets bear names from the Disc World of Sir Terry Pratchett and which had officially twinned with the writer's fictional city of Ankh-Morpork. No, Wincanton for me was a place of false optimism after reading the words of the former mayor who said, "The link with Discworld works extremely well for our town, helping to boost the local economy. I know of three families who moved to Wincanton because of this quirky connection." They must have been big spenders.

Instead, with my family heirloom of a broken black 'Timex' alarm clock in a Tesco bag on the back seat of the car, I had a perfect excuse to head for Orchard Mill. First built in 1613 and tiddled with over the years, it boasts a white-painted house of jaded three storey grandeur and barns that woodworms hold together with monkey-grip, sitting beside the water meadows of the River Swilly. No, not the one in County Donegal, but the stream in West Somerset mentioned in a Saxon document from AD 854 saying Saxon King Aethelwulf had granted a piece of local land to someone or other.

I wanted to see how Bertie and Angela were getting on. Each was having a face-lift in their late seventies. I had also got a tip-off about 'flying-mice' from my friend Phil, a former bat warden from Willett who used to take his son Roger with him on roof inspections. He stopped doing this when an old lady, a recalcitrant council house occupier, grumbling that her loft was very grubby, prompted a four-year-old Roger to pipe up. "Oh don't worry, our attic's full of chicken shit."

So, letting a horse-box rattle away in front of me going nowhere fast, I changed tack and took a left turn in Williton by the brown sign saying 'Bakelite Museum', just beyond the troubled financial bank. Then, following my bonnet, I crossed a cattle-grid and entered a time-warp. I parked between a very large grey tin can and an edible mustard left-hand drive Trabant, a car with heavy eyelids whose name means 'satellite' in German. Hereabouts it was known as 'Oops' and with an engine of only five moving parts, power levels similar to that of a lawnmower and a top speed of 30mph, this Trabbi was the epitome of socialism. Tatty around the edges, not capable of doing too many things, not too efficient, but still manages to work somehow. Made of recycled material like wool and cotton waste from Russia and phenol resins from the East German dye industry, Oops was chompable by sheep and pigs, should they fancy it. From over a barbed-wire fence a couple of golden-brown cows mooed hopefully towards my little grey Skoda, possibly eyeing dessert.

I told them not be silly. Two 1980s plastic 'Itera' Swedish self-assembly bicycles, the preferred brand of transport in the West Indies due to issues of rust, propped against some stonework would, I assured the cows, be much more palatable. I was wrong, however, but that was on a technicality.

I had arrived at 'Planet Patrick', a world of polyoxybenzylmethy-lenglycolanhydride replete with the chucked away and to my generation, the familiar.

The paddleless iron mill-wheel was a picture of skeletal dereliction and a metal MOD sign nailed to thin wooden post declared ' Out Of Bounds To Troops'. A white egret popped its head over the parapet of the riverbank and gave an exaggerated blink suggestive of disbelief. "Bloomin' 'eck, a visitor." Sucking at the air I assured the leggy bird the feeling was mutual and went in search of humanity. My 'Timex', a casualty of a picture frame falling from crumbly bedroom plaster, would surely appreciate the chemistry of such a place. It was the domain of one man, Patrick Cook, a collector, sculptor and boffin who lived in plastic heaven. He was a proven whizz at mending the 'unfix-able', something I had gleaned first meeting him at a New Year's party after the conversation had left the topic of Bertie and Angela.

Wiry, moustached and woolly cardigan under a sports-jacket, Patrick resembled a cross between a fatigued wing-commander and a weary-eyed Bohemian who had stumbled across Soho. He appeared to earn his living from an honesty-box. I found him sat at a garden table in a patch of sunshine furrowing his brow, engrossed in the daily broadsheet crossword and a jam sandwich. Two dogs, Rufus, a golden Retriever, and Toffee, a Norfolk terrier, furrowed their brows, too. "Old fashioned name for a brick. Three letters. Ah, that's a pun," said Patrick.

"Patrick?" I said.

The next answer was of the stock variety adopted through unbal-anced books. "Could be," he replied, not looking up. Then with an upward glance, "Oh, Charles. Like a cuppa?" I nodded enthusiasm, a cue for the sun to go in and allow the March wind to get the upper-hand. He raised himself, flicking at the first wasp of the year. "Ho hum. Go and find Bertie and I'll bring out the tea-tray."

I was honoured. Patrick had a penchant for vintage caravans, well, any caravans really. He had even invented his own that he called 'The Pod', curvaceously plastic, with portholes. It was a small-scale Bicknoller-based workshop operation hot off Channel 5's Gadget

Show and featuring in many a supplement magazine carrying a photograph of Patrick in his favourite 'de-mob' suit. His friend, Sir Clive Sinclair of C5 fame, could have taken off his hat to him.

In the chill, Bertie was a handsome blue and of English crafts-manship. He was a 1932 'Winchester' made out of hardboard by Bertram Hutchings, the Rolls-Royce of caravans born only twenty years after the first horse drawn caravan affair. Inside he was a love-liness. Timber framing aka a Morris Minor Traveller gave cottagey ambience. Above the curtained window perched collectable caravan club china.

"Don't touch!" said Patrick behind me, balancing a Denby tea ser-vice and a picnic. He took to the bed, happy to share with the dribbling salivations of Rufus and Toffee, before his manners remembered me.

Through the window I saw a delight of fairies and a miniature wooden bridge spanning the millstream, crafted by Patrick for his daughter, Sophie. They lay in the shadow of Angela. With leaded windows, green paintwork ticked out in yellow and with red wheel hubs she looked the picture of prettiness. The same age as Bertie, an aluminium shell made her look tougher somehow. Either side of her door were two potted bay trees. Patrick had done a wonderful job and was planning to give a finishing touch of wallpaper patterned with a blackcurrant berry motif, not forgetting a chemical loo.

He was a mine of information. Back in the 1930s caravan sanitation was claimed to be as good as 'city sanitation' and for less than a fiver one could buy the market leader, the 'Elsen Indoor Chemical Closet' on a thirty-day free trial. No need to water-flush and no plumbing. Apparently it was installed on H.M. Estates of Windsor and Sandringham.

Golly.

"I want Angela and Bertie to be holiday lets. I thought people might like them," said Patrick.

They would, without doubt. The cheek-by-jowl caravan cities between Waterrow and Weston made Bertie and Angela the high-lights of Somerset. A cert for Enid Blyton lovers, as long as folk got to hear that both old-timers actually existed.

"Did you see the Slimline Liberty Vogue when you came in? It was at the Ideal Home Exhibition in 1955, you know."

"The grey thing beside Oops? Lovely."

"Really?"

"Patrick, can you mend this?" I asked, remembering the Timex.

Patrick peered into my bag. "Maybe. Come, let me give you hope."

I followed him, leaving Rufus and Toffee licking crumbs, from Bertie to his extensive tuttle that was home. In one of Life's synchronicities a reedy sound came from a transistor tuned into a retro Radio 4 programme. "We are the Ovaltinies / Will you share our joys? /At work and play we're more than keen / Because we all drink Ovaltine, / We're happy girls and boys."

On a kitchen surface sat a small green plastic cabinet. "It's from Damien Hirst's studio. He brought it to me to mend a couple of years ago, but never bothered to come and collect it." How did Damien of tiger shark-in-formaldehyde fame, not to mention sheep and cow, hear about Mr Plastic Fantastic? I mean, for goodness sake, Patrick shuns publicity and never answers emails or picks up the phone. Patrick was a bit off-hand about this, saying something about his ex-girlfriend being Damien's taxidermist and "bits now going off."

He gave the cabinet a pat. "Lucky it's survived, really. I had a little fire in here just when the cabinet was outside drying on the lawn." An understatement. On the wall was stuck a photocopied newspaper clipping that showed evidence of an inferno.

"Bloomin' 'eck, Patrick," I said. "Were you trying to cook a Trabbi? A naïve quip I was to learn because, in order to avoid frustration, a Trabbi is best served raw.

"Don't be unkind," he chuckled, going on to explain that Oops' heavy exhaust particles were not that bad for you and better than some of today's unseen carbon perfumes. He seemed gleeful at the irony that when the Berlin Wall came down twenty years ago it gained the Trabbi cult status among naïve lefties and trendy journalists, too young or stoned to remember the Cold War.

I asked him if he met many journos. "Oh, I think there was one who visited a couple of years ago from the *Telegraph*. She 'cold-called', nosing around with her goddaughter and the girl's family. All very uncomfortable. She asked if I dusted and was overly ... cheery. And she wanted a quote. I told her this was my 'Pitt Rivers of Plastic'."

I nodded, lying knowledge, leaving it until later to google 'Pitt Rivers' and find an anthropology museum in Oxford massively Heritage Lottery funded. With such money washing about why was Patrick so poor? Then again a four-inch plastic black and white figure of a McDougalls flour man, I suppose, doesn't have the kudos of a shrunken head.

Shuffling a pile of post he lucky-dipped one and opened it. 'It's from Gerry King of Zero Lubin notoriety. He's found a 1947 Lincoln in a Grenoble wood. American writer owner and suicide doors. Paris 75 suffix. Been there since 1957, apparently. The steering wheel, door lock stalks and window winder handles are all Bakelite. Look there's a photo. Ooooh." Was this to mean a renewed French connection? The framed photograph of Patrick in a golden waistcoat, leaning against Citroen DS with three Bakelite ducks stood in front of the car's 1970s' number plate DUX 217L, hinted at bygone halcyon days.

As the Ovaltinies were replaced by another tuneful memory, Patrick revealed his fanaticism began when he bought his first radio in 1969. "I saw it in a shop window on my paper round every day," he said. "I bought it on HP for £5. I just loved the material."

Ah, that material. What was the fuss about? Patrick saw it as nostalgia that like Marmite you either love or loathe. In fact it was a twentieth century resin revolution concocted from phenol and formaldehyde that had been the discovery of a Clifton College old boy, Sir James Swinburne, 9th Baronet, the 'Father of British plastics.' James's find was a vast improvement on shellac, a resin made from Thai beetle poo.

Unfortunately, back in 1907 James delayed in getting himself to the patents office. Whatever the reason, nonchalance, torpor, or like Patrick, simply enjoying sipping Earl Grey tea in springtime, he missed the boat. If he hadn't, my Timex might have been made of 'Swinburnite' or 'Knightnite' Instead, Dr Leo Hendrick Baekerland, the son of a Belgian cobbler and a maid, achieved a grubby cube of lemon jelly out of a violent chemical reaction while living in Yonkers, New York. In a rush of Yank style opportunism he was off to the patent office a day before James and the world got 'Bakelite'. James, stiff-upper-lipped, got nowt but a handshake; proving, in the words of Neil Oliver, "Whoever writes history, owns it." Although to be fair to Leo, he did invite James to form Bakelite Limited with him.

Patrick now had the original 1930 Bakelite factory foundation stone. And that was not all. He still had a whole Bakelite factory to unwrap. 'Fairgrieve Bros, Sunderland' had arrived as a history on pallets. There was a whole range of gubbins including a set of antlers, the names of workers clocked in on the last day, and the clock itself stopped at ten past four in June 1955 just as the Liberty Vogue hit the spotlight.

The Bakelite Museum was what it said it was and filled three barn storeys and oodles of shelves with colourful objects used by an older generation between cradle and grave. Indeed, the largest Bakelite moulding was a coffin. However, as Bakelite was renowned for its heat-resistant properties, this didn't go too well at the crematorium. The product became as dead as its occupant.

Others had faired a bit better. Here were toasters and telephones, false teeth and fishing reels, sewing machines and hair-dryers. There was also the stuff of war. A radio had a swastika on the dial and German eagle on the cabinet face. Another, Patrick's favourite, was fashioned in the 1930s like a world globe. A walking stick had a battery-operated light in the tip, a gadget for the blackout made so short that one walked with a limp. Patrick happily demonstrated, before pointing at the dangerously curious. A Williton lady had asked him in the street whether he wanted her table-lamp stand. Of course, he did and went to have a look finding it complete with a light bulb and lampshade. The lady was a little taken aback when he told her the stand was an old wartime incendiary bomb.

Truthfully, it was astounding what he had come across. A set of Bakelite headphones that were heavy and hurt the head, used at the BBC in the old 'Broken Biscuit Company' days would have transported my next door neighbour, Jill, back to her Bush House radio production time in London. Two radar pods from a Lancaster bomber were discovered being used as geranium planters. And the grenade he played with had to have a story. "Must get around to diffusing this," he said. Was he joking?

And there was so much still out there to find. Where would Patrick put it all? He showed me plans for a futuristic, expansive and properly funded Planet Patrick, perhaps in Birmingham, where much of the moulding-powder manufacture of Bakelite happened. But could such a dream, if realised, ever compete with the accepted digestive qualities of Cadbury's? I shook my head in silence.

A shout surprised us both. "Ooh, punters," said Patrick. But, no. It was a buxom leafleter from the cavernous attraction of Cheddar Caves and Gorge, doing a drop of for the season ahead. She wore a printed T-shirt declaring 'Cheddar Gorgers'. "Oh, she is indeed," said Patrick.

"What?"

"Looks gorgeous." Between a rock and a hard place, she might have been.

I suddenly felt a cold sweat come on from a stashed T-shirt related memory of following the Wivey rugby team. Only the week before I had Phil, who's not a young man, in the car as I dripped in several pints of diesel at Junction 27 services on the Devon/Somerset motorway corridor. With my back turned I heard Phil shout, "Excuse me! Can you turn round? I want to read your chest." My neck did an owl in time to see the attractive T-shirted lady, who had been filling a 4x4, looking bewildered but doing as she was told. Her partner, a tattooed monster that had emerged from the pay-station, clenched his fists. When needs must, Somerset can still offer such a bliss of sanctuary. Perhaps, this was why Planet Patrick made me feel so happy.

"Is it 'infra dig' to take snaps?" I said, toying with my memory aid of a baby digital camera.

"No, drinking's not allowed."

"Eh?"

"Schnapps." With a giggle, Patrick left me marvelling at the shocking design of an electric hot water bottle and went off to greet a skirt and headscarf unsteady on a bicycle that gave him a box of eggs and wobbled away again. Despite him being out of sight,

Patrick continued to look at me. His portrait by the contemporary artist of value, Michael Taylor, an old chum from Patrick's Goldsmiths School of Art days, hung on the barn wall. Patrick's face appeared like melting wax with eyes rheumy pools of world-weariness. Painted in return for a 'big favour', Michael, I understood, still owed Patrick another one. Not for me to pry the favour's nature, though.

It certainly didn't seem to be financial. The honesty box had a dusty web over its slot.

By the time we joined up again an hour later I had discovered Patrick's exquisite wood-carvings of a boot, a camera and an 'old-school' telephone. "You've definitely got bats at the top of the barn. Their poo's glittering like fairy dust on your whittlings," I announced. Of course, Patrick knew that. His brother, like my friend Phil, was a batman.

"Pipistrelles. And a Greater Horseshoe flittered into Bertie once," he said.

I told him that I had had recent close-encounters with a colony of its smaller cousins, lesser horseshoes, who made an appearances inside the Servants' Hall of 'Tyntesfield', a Gothic pile near Wraxall built on the profits of Peruvian guano. Proof that where there's muck, there's brass. The house was the brainchild of William Gibbs, who had taken over his father's agricultural fertilizer business, "Anthony Gibbs and Sons', that prompted the popular 1870's jingle,

"Anthony Gibbs made his dibs
Selling the turds of foreign birds."

Indeed a lot of 'dibs' were spent on the billiard room where William, then in his seventies, installed a spectacular, centrally heated billiard table connected to the gizmo of an electronic scoreboard. A player's tally was instantly recorded at the press of a button.

Now Tyntesfield took its cue from bats. Along with lesser horseshoes summer-roosting in the roofs above the billiard room, six other species shared accommodation. Indeed, with the house these days in the caring hands of the National Trust, the bats are considerably catered for. Even essential scaffolding covers have escape holes in it.

As a consequence of all my batty experiences I felt compelled to write a short story, called the 'Angels of Plash' about my friend Phil's cat. "You can read it if you like," I said to Patrick. He gave me one of his looks, suddenly becoming more interested in diary dates.

His Pod's autumn outing was to be at the Montecute Automobile rally. "Come along," he invited. It was an event that followed on nicely from Patrick's planned late summer 'Bakelite Picnics', with period clothes, Bakelite picnic sets, Spam sandwiches and champagne.

In the meantime, I voiced my hope that he could keep body and soul together. "No problem," he said, reminding me about the egg delivery. And little luxuries to keep himself presentable? Again, no problem.

If Oops was a satellite of Planet Patrick, so too was the shop with the red-and-white pole above the door in Minehead's Friday Street. This traditional 'Gentleman's Hairdresser', has been a family business of the Bale clan since 1887. Over all the years they've just moved premises once and that was only from a couple of streets away.

As with Planet Patrick, to telephone is useless. The clan leader David Bale, snipping away with his team of his two sons and a daughter, doesn't allow a phone in the shop. Looking like 'Grouty', the inmate character in the BBC comedy series 'Porridge', David believes in walk-in appointments only. Neither does he advertise. The conversation is of Alf Garnett and modern TV guides offering 'girls in birthday suits and bouncing their bits'. I'm sure he must have a greater repartee, as I only speak from experience. Silence means sitting mind-empty, staring at the reflections of rotating ceiling fans in the ceramic sink as clipped locks tumble.

David and Patrick are kindred spirits in today's hard times, and between themselves have agreed, in a private arrangement, to return to the old-fashioned Somerset economics of barter. At the back of the shop, two large signs of the defunct declare "Visit Minehead's New Swimming Pool Right on the Sea Front" and "Wills Wild Woodbine Cigarettes – More Popular Than Ever". Three walls are taken up with filled glass-fronted display cases exhibiting a barbering yesteryear, like razor straps and shaving brushes, snuff boxes and medicated wadding, yellowed adverts for 'Sprocks German Hollow Ground Razors' and 'C.J King Human Hair Merchant'. None would look amiss on the set of Johnny Depp's 'Sweeny Todd'. Among the paraphernalia are items of Bakelite, so many that David can't remember exactly what, brought by Patrick as payment in kind for a haircut 1940s' style.

Yes, Patrick had best stay smart. The potential was there, what with Bertie and Angela receiving guests and picnic parties, for that egret to seek a quieter backwater. But, then again, interest in the Bakelite Museum seems stuck at the economy rate of nought-point-five percent.

Myself, I couldn't but help an early return for a cup of tea and the Timex. In the kitchen Radio 4 was still at it. 'Today' programme presenter Evan Davis spluttered unsuppressed laughter reporting the saga of one MP's expenses claim for a duck house. Surreal. Only at Planet Patrick, surely?

# The Angels of Plash

Combe-secret beneath Willett tower a rutted buppity-bump track descends to a watery belly-laugh of a stream ford and then up again. The track rises passing alongside a barn once filled with the fattest bats, until it ends at a house called 'Plash'. Here there are bogle-broods, and a phooka hatched in jelly while its father became spirit.

While the phooka twitched Millie's Mum and Dad had become busy with their lives. In doing so they told Millie to believe in Heaven. And so she did. Millie held tight to her belief as she went to live at Plash with her grandfather.

That place of bogle-broods was a strange spot for a merchant to have built a home. Remote. Rambling. Millie had often wondered why he'd done it. Ponds and gardens became her grandfather's scythe-blade discovery. Wonder enclosed within high walls and terraces of stone. Stone cloaked with the ivy weave of time.

Leaning on the stump of a fallen hillside pine tree, Millie would gaze, eyes straining into the dusk, down at her grandfather's home. Above her from a higgle-piggle of nest tangles ravens a-hawed to beckon the night and bats began to flit silent searching. The girl's heart filled with tingle.

Bats eat fairies, Millie's grandfather had said matter-of-factly, as he tended his fruit trees. Millie knew that he was right. It was there to see, plain as day up in the barn loft. Grandfather had stooped to the floor and picked up a dropping with his thumb and middle finger. Bat poo, he'd whispered. Millie stared at the sparkle of reds, blues and blacks, as he crumbled it. Like glitter, she'd thought.

At Plash the fairies were forever hungry. And forgetful. They needed looking after. Millie couldn't see them, but her grandfather could. He could also hear the pigsy-prayers. That's how it is sometimes.

From their branches the fairies dangled. Bat prey. Silver-swinging in moonlight. Damsons and apples, quinces and figs, never forgetting the pears all luscious to eat, Millie overheard her grandfather say with a sigh.

Goggle-eyed gluttons in a moonshine paradise. That's what a phooka thinks. But without phookas fairies have to rely on pigsy-prayers.

How helpful that a phooka takes the form of the first thing it sees. Changlings are like that. But there is a giveaway. A phooka always has wings. And that's how it was in that day of snowdrops down by the pond where the phooka mould lay with a wriggle inside. A jelly-mound waiting to be found. To peer was unwise; to poke, daft.

The silly grey kitten-brained house cat paw-prodded and the jelly-mound wobbled, whilst the hatchling giggled in its slime.

Cats have a habit of finding the most interesting things, just when its person wants them, and bored children have a habit of looking for a playmate. Having searched in all the usual kitten-brained places of bat-barn and potting-shed, greenhouse and stable, Milliewent to look where her grandfather had last used his scythe.

There beneath a wall beside a pond and piles of hackings the kitten-brained cat was staring at an angel stroking another kitten-cat. Millie stared, too. My angel, she thought.

Millie's angel was dressed just like a man she'd once seen in an old painted picture her grandfather had found in the attic. Bewhiskered, wearing a high collared coat with tails. Wise-smiling. But unlike the man in the picture, this man had wings. With a chuckle the angel vanished and two kitten-cats looked at one another. Both grey, both cuddly, but yes, only one had wings. Millie went to tell her grand-father. Grandfather nodded to himself knowingly. It went without saying that Nature has her reasons. Of course, he didn't disbelieve Millie. How could he, when he could see the fairies?

In turn Millie was thrilled to have two kitten-cats to play with. But as the house-cat grew bigger and sillier, the new cat didn't. Millie wondered about that, but most she wondered about the wings. Millie named it Harpy, because instead of purring the cat made a throaty 'har-har-har' and because peas were the smallest things in her grand-father's garden.

Harpy was still the same size when the garden fruits plumped on trees. On a night when the kitten-brained house-cat snug-blanket snoozed and the moon was as bright and round as harpy's eyes, that small grey kitten-cat left Millie's sleep-cuddles and became the girl's delight.

It was a long time ago that Millie's angel found that walls of stone weren't enough to protect fairies, not from the bats of Plash. The bats simply sensed them. Perhaps his daughter could do better, because bats are only flying mice.

So there it was. Millie tree stump stared into the dusk. Staring down at her home. Laughing at the chuckling night-flyer. Darting. Claw-tearing. Paw-batting. Grey furry-guardian of the forgetful fairies who branch dangled in moonlight munching damsons and apples, quinces and figs.

And Millie believed that both man and kitten-cat could be angels and that Heaven was the Land of Harpy. A land of bogle-broods and answered pigsy-prayers, and where a merchant once prodded some jelly.

## JIGGEN
# BRIGHT WORMS & COLD HEARTHS

*"We are all worms, but I do believe that I am a glow worm."*

Sir Winston Churchill (1874 –1965)

Somerset is full of ruins in which stones have absorbed memories, and I love such places. I don't just mean the obvious castle, like Nunney, but the hidden. I'm on about the ones with a pull, from the small scale of Alfoxton's dog kennel to the larger, like the village of Clickett.

So call it 'tuning', but on a day of blue skies and foxgloves a vague comment over a cream tea at Planet Patrick entered my good ear. The chap sipping Lapsang Souchong knew somebody I didn't, who was tinkering with something interesting. A couple of phone calls changed that. Life is all about connections.

Lonely in field near the 'Merry Harriers' pub at Forches Corner and hidden from the road by tall hedgerows for most of the year, yet standing out, some think, like a sore thumb in winter, is a large brick fireplace. Living out of a van on the Blackdown Hills, Tim Staples, a Bristol artist, became intrigued and received a chimney re-pointing grant. Defunct since the 1870s, the stack on Leigh Hill is all that remains of the officers' mess and barracks of the Somersetshire Militia's summer encampment. As a unit they proved to be none too popular. At the time of Monmouth rebellion the Militia took the field with Monmouth. Which was a mistake Judge Jeffries didn't condone.

Also, their name remains infamous in the USA today. The explanation for this was guarded.

The fireplace, now the centrepiece for folk of alternative persuasion to hold drumming festivals, is generating archaeological interest. Tim has unearthed bits of glass and pottery, but nothing with a regimental badge. Nor anything exciting, like brass shell casings.

Folk in rural Somerset seem to like guns a lot. Fox, rabbit, fezzie and little Frenchmen all bear witness to it. Little Frenchmen? It's what the locals call red-legged partridge. Why? Well, take close look, as these small game birds march in regimented quick-time under your car tyres, as you pootle the country lanes. Thousands were imported from France in Napoleon's day and kept their heads down.

Despite many shooting parties whinging that the birds were un-sporting in refusing to fly, the Emperor posed the bigger problem. Napoleon thought to follow the partridge to England with an invasion army. As a result, joining the county's militia became virtually compulsory.

Somerset became an armed camp with men drilling in every village. At Monkton Combe every young man was volunteered; at Ditcheat there were 143 volunteers out of 175 men between the ages of 17 and 55; at Glastonbury every able-bodied man was on parade. It was a demonstration of solid determination that was all too soon forgotten.

Up and along a bit, between Staple Common and Mount Fancy, is Britty, a moss covered farm ruin with a large cold hearth fireplace once a part of a cottage. Evocative and lying secret about a thousand-feet above sea level, the place is among my favourites in all of Somerset. A wellie-land that primary school children dragged their mums and dads to by splashing up a tickling stream bed. This was the legacy of a story I wrote about a snaggle-toothed witch called Maggie Greenteeth, who I imagined must have once lived there. Kids can be so impressionable. Indeed, my own four children loved to play among Britty's stones and shadows.

For my daughters, it was a place of woodland fairies and non-baptised babies turning into butterflies. Maddy and Ez hid in the holly coppice that was the bogles' home and their small hands caressed the tree with holes from where the pigsies peeped. And what to them appeared a tree with bark like clay was a sycamore that now has words about glow-worms carved into it by my friend Michael Fairfax. "You pick them up and they go out. You leave them long enough they come back on again."

These days, the glow-worms once seen on hedge banks on summer evenings, particularly around nearby Neroche Castle, are missing, their magic gone. James Thomson's poetic eighteenth-century lines, "Among the crooked lanes, on every hedge / The glow-worm lights his gem; and through the dark / A moving radiance twinkles," no longer hold true. Pesticides did for glimmering. However, I have come across an small exception to this. In the verge of Withybed Lane at Cucklington, near Wincanton, glow-worms, once known in Somerset as 'stare-basins', are today protected by adoring conservationists.

Britty truths did for my story. Imagine the surprise when it was discovered that Maggie had never lived at Britty at all, but that Ted Rooke had done. The glow-worm words were his and sycamores are legion, growing out of walls that eighty years ago formed Ted's childhood home.

His family had a military background and occupied Britty in the 1920s. Back then Britty had a skyline of scotch pines and conifer plantation, though not as thick as today. By the 1960s the farm fell into disrepair, being finally abandoned in 1975. Soon after it was stripped of useful building materials and left as a ruin with the exception of the cottage fireplace.

Green-wellied, clean-shaven and sporting a grey baseball cap and sunglasses, Ted sat in a portable aluminium framed stool on Britty Common. Twiddling a walking stick with his thumb and forefinger, he chatted into Michael's tape recorder about things within his knowledge, like geese poisoning grass and his grandad's favourite pair of horses, Blackbird and Topsy who had pulled a cow out of a floating mire on Dumpty Field, where you could once make the gorse bushes shake. Recently Ted had delighted in showing his grandchildren the very place and was tempted to either bounce or bog snorkle.

Ted, one of five children, was born in Taunton in 1927, the year his grandfather took on the Britty tenancy, a place with both a farmhouse and a cottage. In Ted's pocket were a couple of old photos.

One from 1911 showed his grandad as a company Sergeant-Major. Although born in Ireland, he had been orphaned and brought up in Bridgwater before escaping to the army, where he was proud of being a pall bearer at Edward VII's funeral. The King had been the Colonel of the regiment.

The other photo was taken in Britty's cattle barton. "We never called it a yard, only the barton," said Ted pointing at himself as a two-year-old sitting on a pony. Behind were a yew tree and the farmhouse. It's the only surviving picture of what Britty once looked like. My children and I just know the 'barton' just as a golden carpet of celandine. Ted treasured the snap, because it showed his dad beside him.

Ted's dad came from Princetown, the son of a Dartmoor Prison warden, a man working at a time when memories were still raw about jittery men from Keynsham and Lyncombe, Temple Cloud and Walcot, Bathwick and Worleigh Manor. Soldiers in the Somerset Militia, none exactly covered themselves in glory during a little known piece of history cupboarded like a skeleton, an incident remembered in the USA today as "The Dartmoor Massacre."

The prison, built by captured French prisoners-of-war, had housed American prisoners taken during the Anglo-American War of 1812-1814. On arrival they were allowed the bare minimum. Each inmate received a hammock, a blanket, a horse rug, a bed, a yellow jacket, a pair of trousers, a waistcoat, a pair of wooden shoes and a cap. After the war ended in December 1814, five-and-a-half-thousand American prisoners were still there, their belongings worn out.

When American prisoners protested about their delayed repatriation, indignant over their continued confinement and angered after being issued damaged hardtack biscuits in place of bread, they staged a loud demonstration on 6th April 1815. The protests were met with gunfire from the 1st Somerset Militia, who had acted as prison guards. Seven POW's were killed and sixty wounded. The militia had fired spontaneously, without orders from the alcoholic drip-drawers of a prison commandant, Thomas Shortland, a naval Captain with a desk job.

One American described the incident as "butchery, barbarity and inveteracy." Prisoner Charles Andrews said it was "murderous" and labelled its perpetrators "bloody butchers" who acted with "cool and deliberate malice." Lord Castlereagh, the British foreign secretary, called it an "unfortunate incident."

At the inquiry, recorded in American State Papers and stored in the Library of Congress, eyewitnesses from the militia such as Sergeant Amos Wheeler and Privates Joseph Manning and Stephen Lapthorn had shrugged their shoulders and said the firing had been personally nothing to do with them.

However, Mike Chamberlain, a prison officer with a penchant for history, gave me a tour of Dartmoor Prison, showed me where the 1815 events had happened and described them in small detail. I saw one Napoleonic legacy for myself. Below a first storey cell window, a cross had been carved into the wall and inlaid with glass by an inmate. It marked where a young prisoner was shot while trying to escape. In my mind the Somerset Militia were guilty as charged.

When malaria caught in India cut Ted's dad's army career short, the family moved into Britty farmhouse. It was there that Ted's three sisters were born. He was told they came from under the gooseberry bush.

For another plant Britty was an Elysium. In spring, thousands of daffodils grew a field. The family used to sell wicker basketfuls of them in the Taunton shop and gypsies also used to pick loads. "But there were plenty for everybody, "Ted said. "Not even one grows there today. Not in the hedges, not anywhere. Cattle have just grazed and grazed and picked them off over the years."

Although there were no deer and very few badgers, foxes brought Ted extra pocket money. If a fox got some hens, as long as he had a pile of feathers to show the agent, he got paid for the bird. It was a good little earner until the Ministry wised up, providing chicken wire instead of hard cash.

Due to the isolation, water came by pipe from a hill spring and school was a sunny walk across Staple common and down into Buckland. Wet mornings, however, brought Ted a three-mile road trudge. His grandad and grandma went into the cottage 'roughing it' with the fireplace, inside which the hooks used for curing ham can still be seen up the chimney.

The family pig was important to Britty life. The last one Ted enjoyed was the biggest of all. "They slaughtered the pig in the pig shed, but couldn't get it out." he recalled. "It was too large. Eighteen or twenty score in pig weight. We always weighed in scores. One score was twenty pound. These days pigs are about six score at slaughtering. With our pig they had to take off part of the rib cage to get it out of the shed and into the kitchen, so it could be scalded."

As a child Ted was fed 'fat bacon' that came off the top of the pig. "We were brought up on it," he said. At eighty-two it did him fantastically well.

In Britty farmhouse, lighting was by oil lamp. Cooking was on the range and a fire was alongside with a boiler for the washing. A mangle did the initial clothes drying and the loo was at the top of the garden. He remembered the difficulty in keeping a candle alight on a windy night. "It helped to fart," Ted said.

The milk from the Rooke's cows was turned into butter and cheese in the alcove outside the back door, where there was a cheese press and racks for the cheeses to mature on. Ted's mum used to make the cheese, Grandma the butter, down in the cottage where there was a butter churn. Each oval pat had a flower design embossed by a carved wooden block and was sold in a shop in Taunton's Tankard Street, owned by one of Ted's maiden aunts, opposite the 'Three Tuns'. Milk was left on a churn stand for collection beside the main gate into Britty at Castle Cross.

In 1941 the whole family had to 'up sticks' to Blackwater, where his father took on the postman's job after a recurrence of malaria. Ted has missed Britty ever since.

After leaving he started work as a motor mechanic and then joined the RAF. When he came out in 1948, he got a job in Bridgwater's ordinance factory and became senior principal foreman, doing development work in South Africa and Pakistan, both very different worlds to rural Somerset. Reluctant to say what this work entailed, he changed the subject, saying that he was "greatly alarmed" how his family was forgetting their ancestry. To counter this, Ted had traced it back to 1530. History needs to be remembered now that Britty's ruins and cold-hearth have been fenced off by out-of-keeping Forestry Commission galvanised steel bar gates and stiles.

And what of the Somerset Militia? Well, they evolved into the romanticised Home Guard in the Second World War. Up on Leigh Hill that officers' mess fireplace will surely look presentable once Tim Staple finishes the re-pointing.

## HAIN JIGGEN
# A BIT OF PLUCK

*"A pound of pluck is worth a ton of luck."*
James A. Garfield (American President 1831-1881)

It was probably as he sat in the bar of the Royal Oak in Withypool writing his *Lorna Doone* that R.D.Blackmore composed Marwood de Winchelhalse's words, "No dog, no man, is a rule here when it comes to work; there is not a man who dare work here without a dog to scare the pixies." He spoke of Exmoor superstition. Lew Pluck works on Exmoor, is rarely out and about without his dog and indeed has been accused of seeing things, although not the little people.

In the shadow of Dunkery Beacon, Huntsman Cottage sits with its outbuildings on the outskirts of Wootton Courtenay. A memorial plaque to a former master of Minehead Harriers, screwed to the wall on a blind bend, reads, "In 1965 Miss Lillo Lumb of Wootton Courtenay gave this property to the Minehead Harriers for their permanent kennels." There was one condition attached to this generous gift, it was supposed to have been anonymous.

But then again the Harriers seemed as incapable of keeping things hush-hush as they were in catching a fox. Since 2004 they have been forced by law to trail after rags. However, their followers are unde-terred. Lew is one of them and never tires of folk asking him, Is that Pluck as in pheasant?"

Both Lew and his best friend Trooper, a golden brown Norfolk terrier, are Exmoor hearted. They thrill to the chase, whether it's from

Selworthy to Minehead's North Hill, or from Dunkery to Horner Woods. Lew's problem was how to keep up. Stocky and barrel-chested, many years of being a Dunster chimney sweep had made him a tad wheezy. Also, there was Trooper to consider. Hunting is all weather stuff and a molly-coddled small shaggy dog is best kept clean. The wind and rain, too, can play havoc.

Lew's solution put pound signs before the eyes of a London based professional snapper. Digital photography, like fishing, is a random art. At a recent Harriers meet at Wootton Courtenay the Barbour clad young woman, who earned her income from snapping the unusual and selling prints off the web, got lucky among the stirrup cup melee outside the Dunkery Beacon Hotel.

Sitting in a home-made wooden box, strapped to a rack mounting in front of the handlebars of a muddy red quad-bike an excited pooch was wearing goggles. It was panting happily with its owner. Lew had got himself and Trooper sorted. Trooper enjoyed the luxury of planting his bottom on a blue-check woollen blanket. There was also a tacked-on blue plastic waterproof sheet to cover him up in the event of downpours.

When the lady photographer offered Lew prints of himself at twenty quid each, he politely declined. Why should he fork out for something he lives with every day?

Indeed, Trooper's box has became a colourful affair after Lew nailed on an Exmoor Ales 'Hound Dog' beer-tap badge. It was cadged from his local 'watering-hole', the 'Forester's Arms', opposite the stone animal pound last used when the Ancient Order of Forester's feasted in the street. The pub was appropriately named. The wooden bar top and the rest of the furniture in the pub was all cut from the same oak tree. And the name was even more apt in the light of the news that Dunster boasts the tallest tree in England. It was measured after a two-hour sweaty, uncomfortable and downright dangerous climb by a forestry student armed with a five-metre long pole and a hundred-metre tape measure.

Coming in at sixty-point-two-metres, which I understand as being one-hundred-and-ninety-seven-feet, the Douglas fir is taller than the London Eye and Westminster Abbey. David Alderman, a spokesman from the Tree Registry, confirmed the student had matched an earlier laser measurement. Nice to have a second opinion, I suppose. But this wasn't all. Dunster can also crow about having the tallest magnolia. However, the village folk shouldn't rest on their laurels for too long. Trees from Northumberland and Longleat are stretching reason.

Anyway, Lew thought his badge a jolly jape. However, it presented a golden opportunity to Jonathan Price, the Managing Director of the Wivey-based brewery, for a user-friendly product marketing initiative in which I have a personal interest. Exmoor Ales were reasonably new on the block.

Whichever way one looks at it, the cluster of Wivey brewery buildings atop Golden Hill dominates the town. And they have done so for over two hundred years, ever since the Hancock family employed half of Wivey's workforce and owned the best of the towns thirty-six pubs. Although the production dwindled to post-war abandonment in 1959, you can't keep a good dog down. Part of the new wave of fashionable micro-breweries, Exmoor Ales moved in and opened for business in 1980. With 'Exmoor Stag', initially brewed as the 'Centenary Ale' for Somerset County Cricket Club, there was market breakthrough from which other brands with a subtle blend of hunting bias, followed.

Thanks to Jonathan's opportunism, Lew now has eight more badges on the box including Exmoor Fox and Exmoor Beast. Lew, however, has a problem with the latter, and thinks it best avoided. The very idea of being carried away by the heady porter is the cause of nightmare. Why? I shall explain.

During a warm, mild evening of early spring, Lew had been watching the first mole cricket he'd ever come across. Not from over the garden gate of his Dunster cottage that opens onto the boundary edge of the village cricket club beside the River Avill, but among the trees of Croydon Hill, where he had been out for walk. Lew thought the standard of cricket was impressive and somewhat unusual.

It has to be said, however, that Lew's discovery was of an accidental nature. He had been attracted by a purring sound, like a sewing machine, that lasted for a minute or two. Croydon Hill is a mysterious place. Children might have believed the noise to be a fairy seamstresses making goblin clothes. Lew hoped the clamour was a goatsucker. Well, he would, wouldn't he? 'Goatsucker' is the Somerset name for the nightjar. Quite common near Lew's home, the bird was once thought to milk goats in the night. Sounds daft, but it was apparently all the fault of Puck, the weird night spirit, who had the habit of sneaking into rural yards intent on making mischief.

Only a killjoy would disagree, or reveal Lew's mole cricket was the bug 'gryllus talpa'. The fact that it can be clumsy and directionless like our Somerset cricket is purely coincidental. Gryllus is Latin for cricket as in 'Jiminy' and Talpa just means mole. To inspect it, the bug makes a good impression of the real thing, sporting a brown body covered in velvety hairs and forelegs with dig-ability. And the true origin of 'goatsucker'? Even simpler. It derives from 'Caprimulgus europeaeus', which translates as European goat-milker and there are a quite a few scattered about Exmoor.

Certainly the mole cricket had confused Lew to the point of sweat. Purring sounds unsettled him. When I turned up at the 'Foresters Arms' at lunchtime, he was in his favourite green sweatshirt with the Harriers logo, sat on a barstool, recovering. It was his habit. Ten years ago he became a local celebrity, overnight. This was down to journalist Chris Rundle from the *Western Daily Press*. "A puma like creature is said to have set up home on the edge of a Somerset village," he wrote.

"Experts are convinced a pride of pumas is prowling the wilds of Exmoor, but now one is understood to have taken a liking to woodland which stretches down almost to houses on West Street. Locals are reporting regular sightings – often only a matter of yards from houses.

Villager Lew Pluck spotted the beast' sunning itself on waste ground near the Forester's Arms. "It was a puma type cat with a tail two feet long," he said. 'Normally, if you were to tell anyone you saw something like this, they would say you had had too much to drink. But this was about 11 in the morning and a couple of other people were watching it with me. A deer carcass was found hanging in the branches of a tree. It must have been dragged there by a big cat, because that's what they do before feeding.'"

It was unfair to discredit such first hand evidence, when a week or so before a big cat was sighted at Capland just off the A358 at Hatch Beauchamp, where the RSPCA have a wildlife hospital. I wasn't sure if anybody had asked whether a patient had been caught out of bed.

Back in the Forester's there was every chance that the hospital would be having something else to look after. From a cage by the door to the loos, Nelson the parrot was causing pain to an unfortunate pool player whose cue seemed at the point of creating parrot kebab.

"Sorry!" called out the landlady, Pam Muirhead, hugging a mug of coffee to her thick woolly cardigan. Originally from Bedlington in Northumbria where the beaches used to be black from colliery coal waste and where the terrier came from, she had in the past thrown out drunks and six-foot-six drug dealers.

Or, had I misunderstood Lew when he had said, "Terry he com in and Pam drug un out." Given that Terry, the local gravedigger was very big and often seen dripping mud, I might have got the wrong end of the stick.

Somehow, though, Pam couldn't quite manage to throw out her five-year-old African Grey parrot. Locals found her logic of the bird being a draw for the curious hard to understand. As parrots went Nelson was insufferable, his red tail feathers a warning sign. He wouldn't go amiss pickled in rum like his one-armed nautical namesake. However, as Lew loved Trooper, so Pam loved Nelson. He was going nowhere.

For me the whole caboodle made the pub a breath of fresh air. That lunchtime we were a motley bunch of bibblers that wouldn't overtax the staff of Pam's lank-haired, fag-dragging hubby, Colin, or her twenty-something fast-balding son, Chris. Terry, clean shirted, his work done for the day, made an entrance with his friend 'George the Overcoat', once an opera singer. In the corner by the cold hearth flopped a tattoo-handed, wall-eyed, scruffy lumbershirt. This willowy artisan was an obvious guddler who had beaten Lew and me to the cider tap by a good margin and was already several laps ahead.

Introducing himself as 'Wezsh', I gathered he was stonewalling up at the castle, which was possibly the reason why the castle's profile looked so full of character.

"Wha' d'ya do?" he slurred looking at me up and down and obviously in need of a plumb-line.

"Oh, you know, this and that. I write a bit. Something about Nelson might be good."

"Wha' ya wri'? Pamphlets? Stuff fer magazines?"

"Nah, books. Book-books, as in chicken but without 'fowl' language."

This set him off. He was in a state, because he couldn't wear his best shirt. That was stained because of the lady who fed the seagulls by the giant, bronze map-holding hands on Minehead's seafront. Flocks of them appeared daily from the town's gardens and rooftops for sustained gatherings "makin' it look loike Trafalgar Square."

"What, like around Nelson's column?" I said, and immediately regretted it. Silly comment. I needed to get back to parrot facts without distracting myself with boat banter that could only lead to hemp from West Coker being made into ropes for Nelson's navy, or his sails being made in Crewkerne. Thankfully, a "bugger off" from Nelson changed the tack, re-focusing attention.

Until recently a regular in the main bar, a bad week saw Nelson consigned to the gloom of the back room. Let out for a fly around, he emerged with the explosive speed of an Exocet to smash a gas lamp off the wall. This he followed up by beak-piercing a set of lips puckered for a kiss and a thumbnail.

Then, obviously, there was the swearing. Nelson had a resource of the unprintable.

Despite the glass-fragments and bared wiring, blood-clots and expressive nature, Pam remains unconvinced that he's a nasty piece of work, blaming the pub's trickle-trade on Tesco's discount shelves. Nelson just needed to be treated with kid gloves, like the sort they used to make at Pittards years ago in South Somerset.

Lew chipped in by saying that there was a lady up on Exmoor, writing for some national newspaper, who fed rats and mice where she lived. "Bloody ridiculous, feeding vermin," he said, finally killing off the subject of Nelson. Or was he? But it was clear Lew wanted an easy life. Just Trooper, and perhaps his several large carp, safe under a heron-proof net in the garden pond.

Newly arrived from east of Frome and odd-jobbing, Pam's son Chris knew about carp, much to Lew's delight. He also liked a bit of hunting and shooting. Exmoor presented a playground and he suddenly announced the intention of going off to try and shoot a stag the following morning. A Bambi breakfast.

Lew, like the rest of us, was aghast. Red, fallow and the smaller roe deer were all common in the woods around.

"You can't do that."

"Why can't you? It's just a wild animal. It's free."

"Because you can't. It's not legal," said Lew.

"Why not?"

"You just can't."

As if on cue, the tension was broken when bearded Michael, the quiz-whiz and a mine of useless information, hobbled in on crutches to pipe up that hyenas have white poo due to their habit of bone-munching. This prompted a further silence of pint-staring awkwardness.

However, this etiquette, common in some pubs and saved for new arrivals, never holds long in the Foresters. Michael, anyway, was cele-brating his release from the orthopaedic ward of Taunton's Musgrove Park Hospital. He wanted us all to know that his survival was down to members of a Masonic Lodge, who brought cans of ale for a couple of their fellows recumbent at the end of the ward. Still full from his breakfast of whisky and Weetabix, he swayed to his feet. "I have a song to sing O," he declared and laid in to Gilbert and Sullivan's *Yeoman of the Guard*:

"Hey-di, hey-di, misery me, lack-a-day-de
He sipped no sup and he craved no crumb
As he sighed for the love of a lady."

Then with a bow, he sat down and retreated back into a world of his own. "C'mon, c'mon" screeched Nelson egging on Ellie, Pam's two-year-old bouncing Doodle with a sock fetish. Seventy-five per cent Poodle, twenty-five per cent Golden Retriever, the dog, in a flight of fluffy puppydom, was devouring a laundry basket casualty. Or was it Terry's beanie hat?

"What's orange and sounds like a parrot?" asked Michael. "A carrot."

Time to take my leave, I thought.

"Have a good day, mate," said Lew.

I would, as long as I avoided Lew's Exmoor Beast during an afternoon stroll on Croydon Hill. Back down behind me Dunster's chimneys were gently smoking, as I went to find a stone-lined Neolithic burial cist that I once crawled into, before my middle-age spread made such curiosity ill-advised. To me the hill had always been a sanctuary of sparrowhawk and buzzard, fritilliary and dog-violet. And now of course, of that mole cricket. In the back of mind, there was also a spot of legend. I would look up the grisly anecdote drawing from a old death-bed confession, when I eventually got safely home.

# The Devil of Croydon Hill

Since the small village of Rodhuish, situated near Croydon Hill in the northern Brendons, had no blacksmith, farmers had to take their implements to Roadwater for repairs. One dark evening, four ploughboys met at Roadwater forge. One was on foot, and carried a coulter that needed sharpening. The other three, who were having their horses shod, played on the superstitious fears to which the pedestrian was prone, telling him he would be sure to meet the Devil as he passed through the wood on his way home.

One of the three then quickly rode to his own cart-linhay to fetch a bullock's hide that was drying there. Wearing this, he went and sat on a gate in a wood through which the lad with the coulter must pass. When the latter reached the gate, there was our horned figure, barring the way.

"Be 'e the Devil or ba-an't 'e?" said the lad with the coulter. Receiving no answer but groans to this reiterated question, he raised the coulter and brought it down on his tormentor's head, splitting his skull. Although the perpetrator was allegedly tried for manslaughter, we are not told whether he was acquitted. What we are told is that at the age of ninety-eight he still believed he had "killed the Devil" some eighty years before, maybe in the 1840s.

(Anonymous, 1925).

# TAIN JIGGEN
# STONED VICARS & PILLORIES

*"Pillory, n. A mechanical device for inflicting personal distinction
– prototype of the modern newspaper conducted by persons of
austere virtues and blameless lives."*

Ambrose Bierce (American Journalist, 1842-1914)

On the first of May young Somerset maidens rose early and went out into the dawn, as they have done for centuries, to 'kiss the dew'. Rubbing their faces in it ensured a beautiful complexion for the rest of the year. These days they're too hung over to get out of bed and a diet of frozen pizza requires more than a dab of a damp grass to remove pimples.

This is probably why some women find Old Cleeve so refreshing. The very nature of the place evokes a vanishing England. And as such, it must surly be worth preserving. Not in the rationale of the Crown Estate Commissioners, however. They had unsettled local trust.

Alongside a blooming camellia, I met a large rainbow-coloured feather duster and a bunch of narcissi carried by a sprightly lady coming down the church path towards me. Intimacy with the gentleman shuffling beside her suggested they were married. Having given me that narrowed-eyed look reserved for strangers both decided I was 'friend'.

"Hello, I'm Jess Tyler," she said, as we exchanged mid-morning pleasantries.

"Think of Tyler as in Watt," said her hubby. "Thankfully my parents did, and christened me A.W. not W.A."

"But the revolting peasants were in the fourteenth century. People have short memories," I said.

"'Not around here," sighed A.W.

"We've just dusted the cat," said Jess, obviously one for keeping up appearances.

'You what?" I said.

Jess looked at her watch and obviously thought there was a moment to waste. So, I learned there's a curious time-worn effigy in the church of some bod no one seems to have a clue about. Locals have been charmed for generations by a sculptured cat with one paw resting on a sculptured mouse at the bod's feet. Some like to believe there's a connection to Sir Richard Whittington of 'Dick Whittington and his Cat' fame. Balderdash perhaps, but the yarn is very nearly contemporary with Old Cleeve's unknown stony-faced chap.

"Anyway, no time to dawdle, go see for yourself. We're off to check on the church hall. They're repainting it. We must check the colour's right," said Jess officiously.

"It's getting misty down there," observed A.W. gazing down passed me at Conygar Tower and Butlins distantly disappearing into sea-fret. Adding with a cough, "We need to clear this moss on the path. Tidy things up a bit."

These were obviously important Old Cleeve obsessives that I'd chanced to meet. However, they were not quite as important as the person I had come to ask about, H.R.H. Prince Charles and admire what folk call the 'Pillory Wall'. Standing along the side of the road with primulas at its base, the mediaeval wall was built of grey stone and mortar. Being four-feet high, topped by an evergreen hedge split half way along by a yew, it wasn't much to look at. But it had become the heart of the community.

In the early 1990s I was filming footage at Old Cleeve summer fete for a speculative news feature that never happened about Randolph Priddy, said to have been Britain's oldest working press photographer. 'Prid' to all who knew him was a humble and self-effacing man of kindness, conspicuous at local events by his unkempt grey grizzle-beard, thick-lens glasses crooked on his nose and battered 'old school' camera slung around his neck. He worked for the *West Somerset Free Press* and lived alone at Roadwater in the biggest tuttle of a cottage I have ever seen, distinctive by its sweet and unchanging internal niff that made polite acceptance of his fruit cake require silent prayer. His home was a Butlins to spiders, books teetered for space with 'box brownie' carcasses and photographic chemicals jostled with crockery. Like Quentin Crisp, Prid was a man who never saw the need to wash-up until a plate "finger-lick-tasted-of-fish." Indeed, his tea mugs were always finger wiped clean. Never ill, he must have been a walking bundle of quietly accumulated microbial immunity.

While Prid did his stuff with the coconut shy and runner duck antics, I told the cake stall ladies to hide the fruit cake and got wind that something was up in Old Cleeve, providing a hot topic of gossip.

It was nothing to do with the vicar Reverend Hugh Allen having his features carved into a hunky-punk by stonemasons during the renovation of the church tower and now seen closer to God high on a crenellated corner. Nor was it related to a prim pensioner telling me for the third time in five minutes how her brother got into trouble with the choirmaster. Such repetition had fully cemented in my brain the fact of the choirmaster falling out with the choirboys and girls. After the nave floor of the church was renewed in 1930 the master found his rustic choristers sitting like angels in the back row of the pews. It wasn't that boredom had killed them, but that each had a recently disinterred skull concealed within the armpit of their surplice. According to the giggling pensioner, the choirmaster "went apoplectic."

No, the cake stall chatter was about the need to solve a problem of heady proportions brought on by the Crown Estate Commissioners. The solution lay in not what you knew but whom you knew. What the folk of Old Cleeve definitely knew was that their lovely time-worn apple orchard in the village centre did not need to be grubbed-up for modern housing and that the Pillory Wall that denied developers access to it should be left well alone. The wall was, many believed, the legacy to the scandalous rhyme:

"There was a young fellow of Cleeve
Who said, 'It is pleasant to thieve!'
So he spent all his time
In commission of crime
Now he's out on a Ticket-of-Leave."

Logically, the Crown Estate Commissioners required sense to be knocked into them, too. However, I learned that nobody had managed to do so. All legally available options to prevent attack from bulldozer and concrete had been exhausted and planning permission had been granted. And after choking on a lump of walnut cake, that was how I had left things.

Now, twenty years later, with Prid having passed on, I was back to find a village with a spring in its step. One of Jess's friends, Jeanne

Webb, from up the narrow lane beside the church, had had a flash of inspiration. She found her best fountain pen and wrote to the H.R.H. Prince Charles asking for his help to protect the ancient site, knowing that he cared about threatened heritage. In a reply by return of post, Jeanne was thanked for her letter and was told that it was being passed on to the Crown Estate Commissioners.

The application to demolish the Pillory Wall was withdrawn and the intention to build on the orchard was reconsidered. After writing a letter of thanks to The Prince of Wales, she received a second letter. This time it sent her his best wishes as well as saying that he was delighted to help "in some small way."

By this time Jeanne was in the mood. She penned a further letter this time to the Crown Estate, setting out ideas as to how the orchard could be conserved as green space. A month later the reply arrived. The Crown Estate was not going to proceed with the housing development. In Jeanne's own words, "it was the answer to all the prayers, hopes and dreams of everyone who had opposed the sacrifice of the orchard. I am proud that words written from the heart, found ears that listened; and that this matter was not too small and unimportant to engage the attention and concern of our future King."

Jeanne was a fountain of knowledge about Old Cleeve and had written a small book around the eclectic hotch-potch of stuff she'd collated. Amongst it all was a story told by a retired villager called Gertie Hodson.

Before WWI in Watchet, Gertie's mum told her she could play where she liked, but on no account was she to go to Old Cleeve, because of the witches. Gertie believed they were the real deal as they had seven white horses and lived in what she called the 'Witches Dome', somewhere along a rustic track between Old Cleeve and Watchet. The witches were said to have caused a lot of trouble and if anyone was lost, it was said that the Old Cleeve Witches had got them. One night the Dome collapsed and "it came tumbling down." By dawn there was not a trace of it left, nothing to show for their long residency. "Proves they were witches, don't it," Gertie decided.

I, too, found things being laid on thick. A couple of thatchers were giving a new lease of life to the roof of a cottage overlooking the reprieved orchard. I recognised one of the guys as Matthew, from Wivey. He and his mate Paul had just bought the business of old Eddie Parks and now called themselves 'Green', which I thought odd due to thatch straw being brown.

However, the work they were doing was in keeping with the house next door. That, too, was newly thatched, but had a pair of beautifully made straw fezzies perched on the ridge. Did 'Green' make such things? I asked, calling up the ladder.

"What?" shouted Paul, before deciding it best to come down for a chat. He was of a new breed. Black stubble like a swaled field, black rimmed designer glasses with just a touch of tasteful orange on the frames and black tea-cosy hat. The worn knee-pads were an essential accessory.

"No," he said. "We haven't made any pheasants, but my cock's impressed other thatchers."

Bit of a lewd chapper, I thought. Paul caught my feigned distaste.

"I've made a large cockerel," he explained, spreading his hands apart in fishy emphasis.

"As big as a pollack?" I said, once more thinking of Prid.

"Yes. Bigger even. I had to tie it to the roof of a Luxborough longhouse with spars and wires to stop it flapping around like a weathervane."

Once back in my car, I gave a thumbs-up as I drove past the men of straw and headed, full of anticipation for the Brendon Hills, knowing that each time Jeanne walked passed the Pillory Wall to church she deserved to feel the cat's whiskers.

# TOTHER JIGGEN.
# PERVERSE ATTRACTION

*"Perversity is the muse of modern literature."*
Susan Sontag (American Writer, 1933-2004)

I had always been intrigued how an airborne plane can shrink a foot in diameter. A Concorde stewardess told me she went from upright to a stoop in seconds. Such modern legends deserved attention. But I was ahead of myself, so impulsively I took a detour off the Langport road just after Fivehead, on my way to the supersonic plane's 40th anniversary at Yeovilton's Fleet Air Arm Museum. I'm sure now, that had I turned left into the RSPSB sanctuary to hide-sit watching nesting herons and egrets for a while, I would have made it to the party, where jet thrusts had no problem in blowing out the candles.

Instead, I felt perverse. By a gothic, wooden, hand-painted sign reading 'Ancient church' I turned right and followed the signpost to Swell. Lo and behold, it was as if I had passed through Somerset's very own portal into Central Europe and lost track of time.

Tall ash trees had branches baubled with heavy mistletoe and a stand of a dozen poplars wouldn't have looked amiss in Chisinau, nor indeed, the corrugated-roofed barn with splintered timber frame that teetered on collapse. Defunct farm machinery brown with rust lay unloved and abandoned among dock leaves and the brittle stems of last year's thistles. Another sign to the church, hanging from a bracket on a telegraph pole, pointed at a manor farmyard of grey stone barns trimmed with details of red brick.

The sign didn't lie. Grey rendered St. Catherine's, dedicated to the martyred Egyptian noble who had a firework named after her instrument of torture, was on the left side of the yard; a tiny church without either bell tower or steeple. It was built about 1450 on the foundations of a Norman predecessor. In truth, there used to be a bell tower, but that was taken down and put in the rectory garden as an ornament in late Victorian times. So now church mice have to put paws over their ears, as bells are rung in the nave.

However, when I sat to cogitate, the church was as quiet as the habit of the aforementioned rodents. I had discovered the timeless. In 1889 Thachery Turner, the Secretary of the Society for the protection of Ancient Buildings had similar notions. "One is imbued with higher feelings and taken back in thought to past ages. There are no modern vulgarisms to disturb one's quietness of mind, and as one sits studying the interior, one becomes more and more impressed by its great beauty." I think I would have got on with old Thachery.

Graffiti was chiselled into the church porch stonework and I could make out the dates of 1589 and 1760. 'Thomas' was carved so long ago that the lettering was stained in yellow lichen. Other words, like those above the slot in the iron bound and sturdy locked oak chest marked 'Fabric Fund', were more recent:

"If aught thou hast to give or lend
This ancient Parish Church befriend
If poor but still in spirit willing,
Out with thy purse and give a shilling.
But if its depths should be profound,
Think of God and give a pound.
Look not for record to be given,
But trust for thy receipt in heaven."

The church registers are in the safe keeping of the Somerset Records Office. There are numerous entries of the passed on being buried in wool. This was a result of economically challenging times back in King Charles II's day. From then until about the Battle of Waterloo six-foot-under body-warmers assisted the growth of the woollen manufacturing industry.

I took a tip-toe stroll, avoiding the souls beneath my feet. A churchyard cherry tree was tied with any number of coloured ribbons indicative of a Swell party. High box hedges were immaculately trimmed and on the other side the fifteenth century manor house boasted new whitewash behind wrought iron gates. But nowhere was a soul to be seen. Not one. I had seen more life in the deepest Carpathians. In Swell the yellow lichen spreads.

Over the parapet of a stone bridge by an old mill, puffy white clouds reflected in the River Isle that had arrived from Ilminster and was slowly on its way to the Parrett. And far away to the naked eye, the church tower of Isle Abbots cut the horizon.

I decided on an amble. This world in which I appeared the only being, looked innocuous enough. Wrong. I barely had time to reach my first puskey breath, before a galvanised steel bar gate suddenly clanged. Startled, my eyes met with those of a squeal-grunting wild boar. With its huge hairy wedge of a head ending in a pointed snout, this was the ancestor of all domestic pigs. And it wasn't alone in unrefined manners. Another twenty or so began gnashing their teeth, trotter deep in a ploughed field. This was my first close encounter with boardom outside the pages of Asterix books. Time to rediscover my motor car, I thought, as the gate was bashed again. Given past culinary experiences these, to me, were beasts more acceptable to Germanic tastes. And even, perhaps, to a wolf.

Call it synchronicity, but how right I was. Around the next one or two bends I was reminded of food. Heavy food. Having spent a month of my life in Vienna, pressed into reducing the tide of thin soups around large submerged offal balls before politeness made me tackle gurt slabs of veal schnitzel, I was prone to the Austrian vernacular. So, too, was the parish church of All Saints in Isle Brewers.

Being ajar, its door was an open invitation. 'Hello, I didn't see you sneak in behind me. I'm closing up in a minute, but you're fine, no pressure," said an authoritative voice that spoke English and introduced itself as Delia Pearmund, churchwarden. After inviting me to sign the visitors' book, she said, "You're my third catch of the morning." I was stupefied.

"Have you seen our Dr. Wolff?" asked Delia, with an insistent look. "He's up by the altar."

Okay, it was dead gloomy, but once again I couldn't see a soul.

Delia tutted. "Look on the wall. At the photograph." While doing as I was told, she told a long story that began by her saying, "Local people flooded from all parts of the area, my apologies for the euphemism, to All Saints knowing that Dr Wolff's services were more entertaining than music hall." However, like after the Levels winter, those floods had abated.

Dr. Joseph Wolff had been a legend in his lifetime and it seemed that Delia had taken it upon herself to send new disciples of his out into the world. Certainly, this explained the scarcity of people appearing this side of the Fivehead portal.

What with the wild boar, it didn't surprise me one iota that the rotund toad-like gentleman squashed into a leather armchair had eaten well during his twenty-two years as the local vicar. Being born in Weilersbach, his life was influenced by the Austrian architectural style. And the church with its eight-sided red tiled steeple, patterned with black tile rings, mostly built by his own money, was his legacy.

During his lifetime Joseph became renowned as "a most remarkable, charismatic and fearless man" throughout England, Asia and India. Born in 1795, he was the son of a Jewish Rabbi. As a young teenager he left home penniless and converted to Catholicism. After extraordinary adventures he came to England, studied at Cambridge and jumped to another horse of faith, the Anglican Church, by which time he could speak fifteen languages fluently. Getting by myself with only German and Romanian out of necessity, I knew Joseph must have been a fellow to reckon with.

He was, and he learned the hard way. At the beginning of the 1820s Joseph began missionary work among Jews and Muslims and finished the decade off by marrying the Earl of Oxford's daughter, Georgiana. After travelling through Europe his sense of adventure took him to Turkey, Persia, Afghanistan, India and Abyssinia. However, things didn't go smoothly. On one journey he was forced to walk 600 miles naked, it's said, in snowy weather. Chilly-willy, indeed. But this didn't deter him. Nor did receiving 200 lashes to the soles of his feet from Kurdish tribesmen.

It was India that nearly did for our masochistic hero. He got cholera. Yet he had more lives than a cat. A doctor restored Joseph to rude health by placing red-hot irons on his stomach. The result was a man with scars on a par with Exmoor's great adventurer Sir Ran Fiennes. Someone who'd removed his necrotic fingertips all by himself in the garden shed using a Black & Decker with a micro blade, picked in his local village after an earlier attempt with a fretsaw had failed. Oh yes, Ran, too, is a toughie. Not even a heart attack and a double heart bypass op four months before undertaking seven marathons in seven days on seven continents could stop him completing them.

"In retrospect I wouldn't have done it, and I wouldn't do it again," Ran had said, before confessing that despite his cardiac surgeon approving the marathons, provided his heart-rate didn't exceed 130 beats per minute, he forgot to pack his heart-rate monitor. At no time did Ran have a clue how fast his heart was beating.

However, whereas Ran does his adventures from North Pole to the top of Everest in the name of charity, Joseph did his to spread the word of God. But in common, both had the attention of Sultans. Ran seconded his SAS experience to the Sultan of Oman who had problems with communist insurgency from South Yemen, and Sultans gave Joseph audience because of his reputation as a world star in the politics of religion, preaching sometimes to crowds of thousands in exotic streets.

It took a "horrendous" journey to Bokhara for Joseph to finally admit his arguments fell on deaf ears. He only narrowly escaped death on account of the Emir laughing uncontrollably at Joseph's appearance in full canonical garb. And looking at his sepia image on the chancel wall, his features were those to which people can invariably be unkind.

So, bringing a little bit of Austria to a quiet Somerset backwater must have suddenly seemed like an appealing project. Certainly it led to a peaceful conclusion to Joseph's life in May 1862. But what made him choose an Isle Brewers 'retirement'? Perhaps it was the realisation the world was incapable of tolerance, too many philosophies of conflict. In Isle Brewers Joseph had preached to the converted.

"Do you like the village?" asked Delia, as I pulled myself away from the aged photograph.

"I think it's a bubble," I said. "Somewhere otherworldly, like Planet Patrick." There in a nutshell was the answer.

"Where?"

"Oh, just somewhere."

Leaving Delia to lock up, I reflected she was indeed the only person I had come across that morning.

Back outside again, wild flowers had opened in the sunlight and I saw a life-size imitation of a white goose sat, neck erect, on a nest of juniper, laurel, holly leaves and teasels that topped a new grave. Eccentricity is still alive and well hereabouts, I thought. But then the obvious made me reconsider. Well, at least Ran was still thriving. And in a Yeovilton hanger was a pink helium balloon, some tinsel and a Concorde-shaped birthday cake.

# FOTHER JIGGEN
# RAISED FINGERS &
# STUMP STARING

*"When a finger points to the moon, the imbecile looks
at the finger."*

Chinese Proverb

In the run up to an 'Ashes Summer' it was June, the 'Honey Moon' month, traditionally the time of year for hives to be full of honey that was fermented and turned into mead. However, though bees have had a mite difficult time recently, less so our county's cricketers. Led by adopted ciderman, the 'baggy greened' Justin Langer, the latest of the line that began with Reverend Stirling Cooksley Voules from Middle Chinnock, they had tasted a recent sweet run of success begun out of sheer cussedness after a Durham wag named Somerset "batting bunnies."

But as the team prepared for an important cup match of hitty-hitty-bang-bang up the road against arch rivals Gloucestershire, there was an acceptance of not being the centre of attention. In celestial sheds at the bottom of heavenly gardens, the gods had made their water bombs and rumble drums and forged their light-ening bolts. Mortals in their hundreds of thousands pointed at the Glastonbury sky, commentators worried about trench foot and two canal boats were spotted on the M5 motorway. This was festival weekend in what Fay Weldon CBE, a Pilton local for ages, called "airhead country."

Marion, aka White Hawk, a tangle of long grey hair, doe like eyes and a dirty laugh might be Fay's proof of the pudding. In this Springsteen year I got introduced to her by chance. Like the gods she, too, plays with water, heading a group called the 'Passion Police'. No, don't misunderstand me, Marion wouldn't be appearing on any stage, be it Pyramid, John Peel or Pussy Parlour, she'd be crowd mingling and promoting her love potion, 'Sex'. Well maybe, love potion is too strong a term, more like an essence concocted by steeping flower heads in tap water for a couple of hours before adding preserving vodka. Quantities of the clear fluid are then strained into pink water pistols that are now ready for use.

"Want some oral sex?" Marian asks random festival-goers and sprays into open mouths.

"Oh, it's such a lot of fun. You should see people's faces," she said. Then confided, "But there is a serious side."

"Really?" I said.

"Course. Laughter helps open up dialogue to relationship issues people have. My essence helps promote healthy connections and in some cases people have found lasting love. Lots have met their husbands and wives through my work."

Such sincerity could be deemed as scary. This being 2009, however, Marion was not the only eccentric deserving of attention.

Within minutes of the first festival wellie mud-splash, food stalls started playing Michael Jackson music. "A tribute type thing," said a chap in a flowerpot hat. Texts were received in tents. The young and the getting-on-a-bit cried, "Oh my God."

President Obama called the megastar, who'd died suddenly in Los Angeles on festival eve, a "music icon", and the communications network became saturated with news desk one-liners: "Charming, polite, childlike man who loved the 'razzle-dazzle' of the circus he knew went on around him." "Eccentric rather than nutty." "Artistic genius on global level." "A man who hated swearing."

My good friend Mark, on the other hand, who'd once 'played' Glastonbury supporting the 'Kings of Leon', was spitting feathers. He had got it into his traditionalist head that Jackson was the antithesis of everything Glastonbury stood for. Aghast at the grief stricken outpourings amid the throng of hundreds and thousands, all Mark could do was mutter, "What are they doing here? Have you heard what they're saying?"

He had a point. A stubble-bearded bloke struggling with his cape of plastic sheeting declared the morning rain as "angels' tears." Then the rain came again, thunder got a big cheer and someone in a Yeovil

Town shirt was looking forward to an autumn clash with new league rivals Exeter City, the only football club in the world to have had 'Jacko' as its honorary chairman.

"Fickle," said Mark, "Just ruddy fickle."

For his part and despite his love of water balloon-fighting MJ probably wouldn't have relished thoughts of Glastonbury. I'm sure Status Quo guitarist Francis Rossi spoke on his behalf by saying, "You've got dodgy, stinky toilets, I don't like those much, and I don't like muddy fields."

This was a sentiment held by many of the Thriller generation who've taken a tip from the Quo living off a bus. With eBay 'smoking' and £500 a 'snip', caravans and campervans are up 98.2% from last year. A fellow named as 'Mr Balls from Essex' spoke for a rapidly growing minority of fans opting to bring their accommodation on wheels. He wanted home comforts like hot water and a shower and added, "We're all getting a bit older and trying to save a bit of money by bringing our own food and drink, so we don't end up spending as much."

I couldn't decipher Mark's comment about such Worthy Farm shenanigans. The feathers were choking him.

In Bristol, fingers again pointed at the sky. Repeatedly. Dismissive gestures to Gloucester Gladiators, who like lemmings rushed to jump off a cricketing cliff. Morris dancers leapt, jingling their bells and hanky waving. Cider flowed. Langer's Sabres were on a roll. Or to put it another way, those sporting brand logos of solicitors, petrochem- icals, car makers and a brewery were being beaten by lads sponsored by a Templecombe egg merchant. To be a 'Yolk-all' was fun. The reason for the carnage, a local sage thought, was that the ball 'swung'. Why this should be met with a glum shrug.

To be fair, the swinging phenomenon befuddled even the best scientists. For example, take the ball Sir Ian Botham bowled with in 1981 when Jacko first sang 'Billie Jean'. He took five Australian wickets for one run in twenty-eight deliveries and caused much head- scratching. After the match Sir Ian gave the ball to his late father Herbert, an aeronautical engineer, to "play with." Working at Westland Helicopters in Yeovil and having access to a wind tunnel, Herbert in turn passed the ball on to the boys there. Despite doing rigorous tests they couldn't find any reason why the ball had swung so prodigiously. Perhaps, it was just Somerset magic. Ironically, Sir Ian hadn't even wanted to bowl and had to be persuaded.

Watching a highlights video at Taunton's County Ground years later, 'Botham's Ashes' still gave tingles of delight to a bunch of volunteers that included me. However, there was no commentary sound. That was supposed to be given by us. We were doing a sort of rehearsal to see if we were any good, before a special hut was built. The idea was that blind people or the partially sighted would be given handsets when they entered the ground and could listen to us wittering.

My friend Mooseman had told me we needed to paint a picture in words. We also got a free meal and could enjoy the cricket. "Put me forward," I said. The rehearsal was crazy. Highlights have difficulties. Just as we were sorting out field settings, next second someone was bowling and was hit, next second another person was bowling and was hit and we said, "Woah!". As I floundered, trying to recall the names of the main protagonists, one bloke remembered the name of the blooming umpire as well as every 'baggy green' capped Aussie.

I suppose with the cap having such iconic status, anyone awarded it, whatever the era, is a name worth knowing, especially if they catch local attention. Indeed, Australian Prime Minister Kevin Rudd said of Somerset's present skipper, "Few cricketers have worn the baggy green with such immense pride and distinction as Justin Langer."

And of the 'few' there were others that graced the County Ground. Stephen Waugh, for instance, and more recently, Ricky Ponting. And of course there was Greg Chappell. Youthfully signed in 1968 he played for Somerset for a couple of years, before emerging as the imperious Aussie batter of the 1970s. On returning to Somerset with the Aussie touring team in 1972, Greg's baggy green made it into the local news years later. It appeared that he had given it away and a local policeman who'd 'found' it wanted to personally return it. Chris Read discovered the cap with the initials 'GC1' inside in Bridgwater over twenty years ago, while searching the home of a suspect during a police enquiry. The owner, who was eliminated from the investigation without charge, told him he had won the rarity in a raffle.

Chris checked who was on the Australian tour in 1972 and the only person with those initials was Greg Chappell, regarded as a generous man by his Somerset colleagues. So to have made a gesture of giving someone the cap for a raffle was in keeping with Greg's character. When Chris retired he bought the baggy green from the Bridgwater chap.

The problem was Chris met the former Australia captain 'down under' and Greg couldn't remember giving the cap away. A mystery remains that no cricketing sleuth can solve.

However, what has come to light is that Somerset's come a long way since the club was formed haphazardly in Deb'n in 1875 with a resolution declaring, "There shall be no county ground." Change though, as we now know, is part of evolutionary life. Today, Bicknoller's Harold Gimblett, Somerset's greatest home-grown batsman, has the little hill in front of St. James's church named after him that could have been the work of a dozen muddy-wants in an afternoon. Sets of gates honour Sir Vivian Richards and Joel Garner. Stands are dedicated to Sir Ian Botham and Marcus Trescothick, and the newest of Somerset's triad of pavilions, muted as a triage of quality, acknowledges Andrew 'Caddy' Caddick.

Indeed, as Somerset took the field from the 'Caddy shack' for the first time in a Championship match, Caddy also found himself playing. Spring pastured in Clevedon and Wiltshire, he was back in the side for his first game of the season and Yorkshire were batting. It was to be a poignant first morning's play. The Tykes were without Michael Vaughan, the Captain of England's lion-hearted Ashes winners in 2005, who minutes earlier had announced his cricketing retirement.

Among the straw hats, walking sticks and broadsheet crossword mutterings, the first trays of pints slopped in under hands of eleven o'clock drinkers. The crowd was building, building. Well, sort of. Two workmen in hard hats leaning on the top balcony rail of the ground's new flats showed no signs of building anything, content, as they were, to stump stare.

"This broadcast is brought to you by the Royal National Institute for the Blind," said the dulcet tone of Richard Walsh, blue short-sleeved shirt and striped Somerset tie to a growing band of listeners both at the ground and listening through internet stream.

Inside our hut it was the sweat that streamed despite the best efforts of a whirring desktop fan. We were sat at the foot of the Ian Botham stand looking out across the twin churches, from a cramped timber-slatted 'potting-shed' whose 'Monkton Elm Plant and Pet Centre' sign-work emblazoning the front made me feel like an exhibit behind glass.

Semi-retired and armed with binoculars and a pocket crib book of cricketing facts Richard was an indispensable "bit of a freelance." On top of a two-hour commentary slot he sorted out the match score-cards, organised the programmes and wrote "odds and sods" for the Western Morning News.

Richard anxiously reported the disturbing scoreboard as Yorkshire's openers breezed through the first half of the morning session.

Then, wicket! Joe Sayer, bowled Alfonso Thomas 8, Yorkshire 24- 1. The Caddick pavilion offered an extended walk of shame. Moments later Alfonso sent down 'chin music', a bouncer cracking a Yorkshireman on the bonce, bringing giggles from a smattering of crowd and a geriatric cry of "Off wiv 'is 'ead."

"Ooer," said Richard. "We'll get an unsporting reputation again."

As a bleeding ear received attention to the delighted cries of wheeling seagulls, Richard and I swapped notes on a blacker day in Somerset sportsmanship, turning our reference books back to 1919 and an inauspicious tie. Sussex had travelled to Taunton short of a player and Harold Heygate, there as a spectator, was pressed into service. Since his last first-class cricket fourteen years before, though, he had sustained leg wounds during the war and suffered badly from arthritis.

Somerset and Sussex scores were level, when the ninth Sussex wicket fell. At that point, there was a hiatus. Historical account then has Heygate with pads strapped on top of his blue serge suit making a valiant, but fruitless attempt to reach the wicket from the Old Pavilion. After some minutes had elapsed without Heygate appearing to bat, someone on the Somerset side appealed and the umpire, a respected Test match official, ruled that Heygate was out, timed out. The stumps were pulled up and the match was a tie. Heygate was recorded as "out, absent". The decision caused controversy in the press and elsewhere, much of it focusing on the lack of civility to a wounded ex-serviceman.

From the shed I witnessed more contemporary struggling. Yorkshire belligerence had seemed to wear out Caddy in the field deep. When the chimes of St. Mary Magdalene church welcomed his first over after long absence, Yorkshire supporters greeted the ball thumping into the boundary boards below a stand with as yet no name. It was an early exchange that over of four days saw over 1600 runs scored and culminated in a day of brilliance. By its end Yorkshiremen wanted to leave their team's coach in a Taunton pub, while they returned to plant potatoes in their home pitch of Headingley.

The star turn was Somerset's heavily tattooed Peter Trego who played the innings of his life that climaxed to one of those sporting days when those present are proud to say "I was there." Peter's 54-ball century of biff-boff-bash enabled Somerset to pull off one of the most amazing County Championship wins in their history. A victory by a margin of four-wickets. It was the second highest successful run-chase in the 145-year history of the County Championship with the home side reaching a massive target of 476 with 4.3 overs to spare.

You have to go back to 1925, when Middlesex made 502-6 to beat Nottinghamshire at Trent Bridge to find a bigger winning total by the side batting last in a Championship fixture.

So no one who was at the County Ground is likely to forget the game or Peter's incredible clean hitting, which brought him 9 sixes and 6 fours in his 103 not out, coming in at number seven.

The only television replays available from Somerset that day were from Glastonbury's 'Pyramid Stage' showing Bruce Springsteen singing Joe Strummer's 'Coma Girl': "I was crawling through a festival way out west ... and the rain came in from the wide blue yonder." But with gritted teeth, the water-gods in a white-knuckle ride had been kind, holding on to bladders strained since the festival's first morning. Within moments of the players leaving the field the gods finally had to let go. The heavenly cloudburst would have thwarted legend, had it happened a few minutes earlier.

Justin Langer called the victory "a bit of a miracle", while Peter attributed his dramatic innings to "a few verbals" from Yorkshire seamer Ajmal Shahzad. He told the club website: "When I first went in, it was uppermost in my mind to just stay there, because I haven't been in the best of form in red ball cricket. Then Shahzad started winding me up and suddenly the ball turned from a pea into a balloon. I decided to let him have some!"

And so he did, swinging from the hip to record the fastest first class century of the season. With the considerable help of 'Marco Tresco' and Arul Suppiah, Somerset's effort was the fourth highest run-chase in first class cricket in England and the eighth highest in the world.

Given guidance from our embraced baggy green, Somerset must surely, I thought, have a sporting chance of a cup, even perhaps a first ever Championship. Just so long as nothing's given away. An Ashes Summer is fickle, indeed.

One thing, however, remained unresolved after that Yorkshire day. What to do with the stand with no name? Surely a chance for an Aussie christening? Then again, what about Sunil Gavaskar or Martin Crowe, actor Russell Crowe's cousin? Where does one draw the line? Well, perhaps below Reggie Ingle, a Bath solicitor with a reputation for taking on and winning cases for the gipsy community and who captained the county in the 1930s, of whom they say he could swear for five minutes without repeating himself.

Memories fade from not just myself. The loudest shouts were now for Weston-super-Mare's Peter Trego as Jacko sang on somebody's radio, "Don't' blame it on the sunshine." Those listening to the broadcast from the 'potting shed' heard a jingle declaring that Blackacre Farm free range eggs were "blooming lovely".

# FULL SCORE
# END PIECE

*"If your knees aren't green by the end of the day, you ought to seriously re-examine your life."*

Bill Watterson (American writer and illustrator, b.1958)

Players and their families from the Somerset cricket team were in Taunton Starbucks. "Good game yesterday," said my son Felix, working 'on bar', to his friend Max Waller, ex Millfield School and a new leg-spinner of fingers-crossed fortune.

"Not so much for me. Got tonked and dropped a catch," confessed Max, knowing that 'sitters' didn't just sip coffee.

"Doesn't matter. It wasn't on the telly," Felix replied

Eavesdropping, Justin Langer raised his lips from a Cappuccino. "Oh, yes it does," Justin said. A week or so later he was to become the highest scoring Australian batsman of all time, beating Sir Donald Bradman's long standing record, during a century at Worcester. That wasn't on the telly, either.

Of course, Justin was right. Values do matter. Taken as an allegory, he spoke for every Somerset heart, even adopted ones, in every cow corner and to each compass point of the boundary edge, from Exmoor to Bruton Forest, from the Mendips to the Blackdown Hills.

I'd say more, and there was much, much more, but my fishing rod was in danger of catching a cobweb. I was in danger of catching swine flu. In the 'Bearin' Up', the bibblers, knocking back fermented fruits rather than caffeine, thought it time to rebuild castle sanctuaries like Englishcombe's Culverhay or Merryfield in Ilton. Each bibbler, however, dolefully accepted pigs might fly.

For me, somewhere out in Porlock Bay hobbit sharks waited to play. Either that or slip into the 1950s' ennui of Evelyn Waugh, who from his desk in Combe Florey wrote, "My life is really too empty for a diarist. The morning post, the newspaper, the crossword, gin."

There are always more ways than one of surviving another Somerset year until time eventually catches us out.

As I tip-tip-tap to a close, the 'take-in-cut-out-and-pass-on' snippet cultured garner obituaries to Harry Patch, the Somerset plumber and last British survivor of the carnage of the Western Front, who at the age of 111 had peacefully passed to a place beyond the freedom of the City of Wells and the dream world induced by counting sheep.

He had departed just before an England Ashes win on a golden evening at an oval east of Frome.

# APPENDAGE
# LOCAL VERBAGE

| | |
|---|---|
| Aarr: | Yes |
| Addle: | A pus-filled swelling |
| Aggy: | Gather eggs as in "I be gwain aggy." |
| Alice: | Ulcer, so be careful when christening your daughter |
| All to lippets: | Fallen to pieces |
| Amper: | Pimple |
| Ann Summer: | More handsome, and nothing to do with sex aids. |
| Ballyrag: | To scold, tell off especially with foul language |
| Baven: | Faggot of unprepared twigs and branches |
| Begrumpled: | Offended |
| Benapt: | Left high and dry by the tide |
| Betwaddled: | Confused |
| Bibber: | Shiver |
| Bibbler: | One who enjoys a pint or two |
| Biddle: | Beetle |
| Bim-boms: | Church bells |
| Bloody-warrior: | Wallflower |
| Boggler: | A horse given to stumbling, but not falling |
| Bucket and chuck it: | The outdoor toilet |
| Bull-beggar: | Hobgoblin |
| Bum-towel: | Long-Tailed Tit |
| Bunches: | Word of exclamation like rollocks |
| Caddle: | Confusion, muddle |
| Chapper: | fellow, chap |
| Clinkerbells: | Icicles |
| Cleeve: | Steep slope |
| Colley: | Blackbird |
| Crousty: | Ill-tempered |
| Dabster: | Expert |
| Daddicky: | Rotten |
| Daddygranfer: | Woodlouse |
| Dang I: | Well, I'm damned! |
| Daug-tuy'urd: | Knackered |
| Dazzy-snoo: | Definitely |
| Deb'n: | Devon |

| | |
|---|---|
| Dewbit: | Breakfast |
| Dimpsey: | Half lit, at twilight or dusk |
| Dinnum: | Didn't they |
| Dirsh | Thrush |
| Dish-washer: | Grey wagtail |
| Down-come: | A fall in income |
| Draffit: | Vessel in which to collect pig swill |
| Drang: | Alleyway |
| Driggle-Draggle: | In a slovenly manner applied to a woman's dress |
| Drowner: | Employed to cut osiers in the dykes of Sedgemoor |
| Drowning the Miller: | Pouring too much water to make the tea too weak |
| Emmets: | Tourists in large numbers |
| Emmet-batch: | An ant-hill |
| Evet: | A lizard |
| Fairy: | A weasel |
| Farty: | Forty |
| Fezzie: | Pheasant |
| Fuz-pig: | Hedgehog |
| Gallybeggar: | Bugbear, hobgoblin |
| Ganny-cock's Snob: | The long membranous appendage at the cock-turkey's beak |
| Gawk: | Stare |
| Git: | Gate. So don't be alarmed if anyone says they're off to hang one |
| Goozegogs: | Gooseberries |
| Grockle: | Tourist |
| Grockle shells: | Caravans |
| Guddler: | A heavy alcoholic drinker |
| Gulch: | Swallow fast |
| Gurt, girt: | Great |
| Hayty-tayty: | Seesaw |
| Hellier: | Roof tiler |
| Hoon: | Throw with vigour |
| Horse-stinger: | A dragonfly |
| Hully: | A peculiarly shaped long wicker trap used for catching eels |
| Hunky punks: | Gargoyle |
| Jack-o-lanterns: | Will-o-the-wisps, the souls of unbaptized children |
| Kern: | Turn from blossom to fruit |
| Lants: | Sand Eels |

| | |
|---|---|
| Larn: | Teach |
| Maized: | Mad, insane |
| Mower: | Moor |
| Mud-horse: | A type of sled with a ski-shaped base and wicker basket used on the Somerset coast for fishing |
| Muddy Want: | Mole |
| Mugglin: | Struggling |
| Narry: | Narrow |
| Nestle tripe: | Runt, especially of pigs |
| Nottled: | Really cold |
| Numbriller: | Umbrella |
| Pew Moanier: | Pneumonia |
| Pink-twink: | Chaffinch |
| Pixie led: | Simple minded, crazed |
| Praper: | Excellent |
| Puggle 'eaded: | Drunk. Cider drinkers can often be recognised by their rosy faces and inability to articulate. They are then considered puggle 'eaded |
| Rampin: | Raving mad |
| Rain-pie: | Woodpecker |
| Ruckles: | Peat stacks |
| Scollared: | Taught |
| Smeech: | Smoky smelling |
| Snap-jack: | Stitch-wort |
| Stare-basin: | Glow-worm |
| Sumshus: | Lovely to eat |
| Tarble: | Terrible |
| Teetsy-totsy: | Cowslip |
| Titty-todger: | Wren |
| Trow: | Sailing barge designed for use on the River Parrett |
| Unket: | Uncanny |
| Viddy: | Right |
| Wevet: | A spider's web |
| Whister-twister: | A smart blow on the side of the head |
| Wopse: | Wasp |
| Wontwiggle: | A mole tunnel |
| Yes: | An earthworm |
| Zummat: | Something |
| Zummerzet: | Somerset |
| Zyve: | Scythe |